THE
24
HOUR
RESET

The 24 Hour Reset © 2023 Jonny Stofko

All Rights Reserved. No part of this book may be reproduced in any form or by any electronic or mechanical means including information storage and retrieval systems, without permission in writing from the author. The only exception is by a reviewer, who may quote short excerpts in a review.

This is a work of non-fiction. The events and conversations in this book have been set down to the best of the author's ability, although some names and details may have been changed to protect the privacy of individuals. Every effort has been made to trace or contact all copyright holders. The publishers will be pleased to make good any omissions or rectify any mistakes brought to their attention at the earliest opportunity.

Printed in Australia
Cover and internal design by Shawline Publishing Group Pty Ltd

First printing: October 2023

Shawline Publishing Group Pty Ltd/New Found Books
www.shawlinepublishing.com.au/new-found-books/

Paperback ISBN 978-1-9228-5051-5
eBook ISBN 978-1-9228-5058-4

Distributed by Shawline Distribution and Lightning Source Global

 A catalogue record for this work is available from the National Library of Australia

More great Shawline titles can be found by scanning the QR code below.
New titles also available through Books@Home Pty Ltd.
Subscribe today at www.booksathome.com.au or scan the QR code below.

THE 24 HOUR RESET

JONNY STOFKO

ALSO BY JONNY STOFKO

Ungoogleable: The Success Secrets of Modern Day Giants

DEDICATIONS

This book is for my family, friends and clients.

ACKNOWLEDGEMENTS

I want to thank my friends, family, clients and connections on all social media channels, you have all played a major role in my journey and I thank you graciously for that.

WHAT IS SCIENCE?

Science: NOUN: the intellectual and practical activity encompassing the systematic study of the structure and behaviour of the physical and natural world through observation and experiment. Anything that can be studied and measured.

WHAT IS BRO SCIENCE?

Bro Science: NOUN: a term for misinformation circulated among mostly men, usually bodybuilding claims not backed by science.

Example: Dude! Drink this fitness tea, it's packed with electrolytes, so you know it's good—they've done studies you know? Sixty per cent of the time it works, every time.[1]

---

1 Anchorman, 2004

WHAT IS MY SCIENCE?

My Science: NOUN: the intellectual and practical activities encompassing the systematic studies of the structures and behaviours of my clients throughout the last six years. Results achieved via my own proven techniques on how to enhance the mind and the body using natural and holistic approaches. Anything and anyone can be studied and or measured.

INTRODUCTION

IT'S ABOUT TIME

A while ago on my podcast I had the privilege of interviewing author Robert Greene. He features in a chapter of my first book but this has nothing to do with that and everything to do with his fixation on 'Life Mastery'. Robert was so infatuated with the idea of human potential that he wrote a book all about it, aptly called *Mastery*.

Here's a little secret about the book writing process: most writers will attest that throughout the journey of writing a book one will experience many different emotions. None of them more frustrating than what I call the ever encompassing, 'Doubt Phase'. This occurs when you're nearly finished with a project and start sharing concepts with people in your circle. It's always the ones you respect the most who give you the harshest feedback. Don't get me wrong, when you find these people, cherish them; brutal honesty is always worth more than the protection of one's ego.

What started out as a book and guide on "body transformations" quickly took a turn when I received an email I was waiting for in relation to "feedback". I sent the manuscript out to roughly ten of my peers and colleagues. One of the common questions I kept receiving forced me to change my entire angle and stance. The response(s) simply stated: And then what? Where's the value if I'm not willing to change?

I thought to myself, *Damn, they're right.* Now this message is only for gym goers; it's basic. It alienates an entire population who've never stepped inside of a gym. I told myself, *These are the people I want to help. How can I make this work for people who don't go to the gym?*

I was frustrated. I'd thrown nearly three months of my life down the drain working on this project, figuratively speaking. I walked away from it for almost five months, and it wasn't until I revisited my old friend Robert's book *Mastery* that, it hit me like a lightning bolt; this book wasn't going to tell the story of how others transformed their bodies and minds, it was going to tell the story about how *you* can transform your body and mind. The vision became clear. In this book I will teach you my systems and habits that are applied within the home, not outside of it. Practical daily actions myself and my clients implement every morning.

I started doing math. What math you ask? Robert's math and every other scholar out there who has tackled the subject of life mastery and expertise. In *Outliers*[2] Gladwell says the only way to truly master your craft is by expending 10,000 hours or more honing and developing it. True story, I pulled out my calculator and notes. Thank God, I'm a bit of a packrat when it comes to my journals. Since 2015, I've written down

---

2 Gladwell, 2008, p. 40.

every single one of my private one-on-one coaching sessions complete with the date, the client's name, their goals and their programming. I have four thick journals filled from front to back complete with all the data that I was looking to self-verify myself with.

What does 'Self-Verify' mean? I'll help you out. Self-Verifying is something I do when I'm asked to give my expert opinion. I ask myself, 'Are my qualifications strong enough to honestly give a complete and valuable stance on the topic?' For instance, if I'm thrust into a heated online debate involving upcoming boxing matches or the next big MMA fight of course I'm jumping in; combat sports are my bread and butter. I've watched every UFC fight since '93 and my boxing intellect dates to the Sugar Ray Leonard era. Now, if I'm asked to give my stance on the upcoming political elections I will humbly always decline. My father raised me to never engage in public debates involving religion or politics. I can't honestly tell you I always listen to his advice, but I do my best.

Back to the data. I started tallying my total sessions each week along with the time spent outside of the session that I used to create each client's individual training program. I added up the workshops I'd completed, along with the total amount of hours I spent lecturing and teaching. It's funny to be writing this, trying to reconstruct the story and attach the humorous emotions I was going through. I was thinking to myself, please be 10,000 hours. As if it were under the mark, I wouldn't be qualified to write my own book? It's funny the mental games we play with ourselves.

The numbers panned out as follows: I broke down the six years I've spent coaching in Australia into weeks, months, then years.

I spent 36 hours a week with clients plus another 18 hours of programming. That's 54 hours a week or 216 hours a month or 2,592 hours a year. Now multiply that by 6 and voila! I totalled 15,552 hours. I made it! By the way, even if this only equated to 8,000 hours, I would have still written this book—I just wouldn't have been so confident about my systems and approach.

A few more things before we get into this book: I'm a very passionate person and I'm unapologetic about it. I've lost friends because of it, and in recent years I've somewhat isolated myself. I have never shaken the feeling of frustration and confusion surrounding my own purpose. I spent years crying at night, praying to forces I probably didn't even believe in to send me the answers I was desperately searching for.

My younger years were spent excelling at everything (I'm not bragging here; I'm simply painting the picture so you can understand my path and hopefully empathise with my frustrations). As a young boy and teenager, school and sports came easy to me. I studied, but not as much as I could've, and I still got all As on my report cards. I excelled at every sport. I would often get embarrassed when my parents would brag about me to their friends. We had a small shrine in my house of trophies I'd won and paper clippings from local newspapers who'd featured me. The only validation I sought was the admiration from my performances on the field or in the classroom. I was a kid who was told by my parents and coaches I'd always be a ballplayer and I loved that. I believed it too.

What happens when reality sets in? When you realise, you're average, that you're not good enough to be a professional athlete? Well, in my case, I turned from a carefree teenager to a stressed out self-medicated young adult. This was where my longing for purpose began. I spent my twenties, an entire decade, wishing for a sign or direction. I had no idea what I was supposed to be doing, and with sports removed from my life I was left without an identity. I was left searching for answers to questions like, What the hell am I even good at?

These were trying times, but I wouldn't trade them for anything in the world. When I tell you I'm passionate about coaching, this is what I mean. The day I coached my first client, I knew this was what I was going to do for the rest of my life. I was going to help people.

WHAT IS A HABIT?

Habit: NOUN: a settled or regular tendency or practice, especially one that is hard to give up.

'You are what you repeatedly do. Excellence is not an event; it is a habit'.
— Aristotle[3]

Let's clarify something. This isn't a business course or a "how to get rich quick" seminar. I'm not selling you anything, and I'm not telling you I have the "secret knowledge" that's going to miraculously change your life. I don't believe in bullshit. I'm not a fan of schemes, fads, trends and gimmicks. I don't possess any supernatural powers. I'm not going to yell at you and tell you to hustle.

I'm frustrated. I'm sad and I feel defeated. My emotions are a derivative of the countless number of friends, family, and colleagues I've lost to multiple chronic lifestyle diseases, all within the last few years. Lives that could have been saved; deaths that

---

3   As cited in Martin, 2006, p. 22

could have been avoided. We're not supposed to die at thirty-nine of a massive heart attack, due to obesity, like my childhood buddy, Nick. Fifty-eight shouldn't be the age you lose your father, like I lost mine, due to a sedentary lifestyle. He should still be alive, and Nick should still be alive. I'm not alone; I'm sure you have similar stories to mine.

There's an epidemic going on throughout the world. It's an illness that has managed to sweep across the globe. Symptoms include: lethargy, laziness, confusion, lack of interest, loss of hope, and obesity. We've lost our way. We've become more connected with devices than we are to our own bodies. We care more about celebrities than we do about our friends and family. When did this happen? How did this happen? Somewhere along the line we've become disinterested. We've forgotten how to love ourselves.

This is the message of this book: You have the power within yourself to make a change and I'm going to show you how. I want to share with you a few systems I use every day, that my clients use every day to live an enriched and healthier day. Hopefully, you will start using them too and they will enable you to have the kind of day you want. Not life, but *day*. Twenty-four hours. That's it. That's all we really have anyway, right?

Focus on what you can control. There's no point in looking back and seeing how far you've let yourself slip. Who cares? I don't give a shit about how much weight you've put on in the last ten years. What I do care about is, what are you going to do about it, today?

Forget the past, forget your mistakes. You are not your failures, or your successes. If they happened yesterday, then let them go. Good or bad, just let them go. Focus on right now. Do this every day. It's a mantra I use with myself and with my clients. It's a mental framework that keeps us focused and committed to the present moment. ISD1MF which means: It's Still Day 1 Motherf#$ker.

No one cares how well you did last week. Nobody gives a damn about how much weight you lost last year. What are you going to do *today*? I ask myself this every morning when I wake up, it keeps me grounded and focused. Every day is day one. There's twenty-four hours in each day, whether if it was great, or if it was awful.

In this book, you will learn the mental hardware for how to wake up every morning and simply hit the reset button. This isn't about anyone other than yourself. I don't want you to share this with your friends, I'm not asking you to tell anyone about these systems. I'm challenging you: how many days can you put together in a row executing these habits?

A wiseman once said, 'We become what we do[4].' What will you become? That's a question that should scare you. Imagine yourself at your full potential. Have you ever been there before? You're not alone if you said, 'No.'

This is the bit that breaks my heart, knowing so many people will live their entire life never truly feeling great, never knowing what it feels like to be healthy. It is possible. You don't need magic pills or crash diets. You don't need secret cheat codes or plastic surgery. All you need is you, and a slight shift in your daily energy expenditure.

Having a plan of attack is crucial for any successful task. Why are so many of us living lives with little to no structure? Is there a link between unhappiness and misdirection? I think there is. I'm convinced there is. I'm writing this as living proof that

---

4   This quote, or variations of it are attributed to a couple of different people: Chiang Kai Shek, Eduardo Galeano and Sean Covey. While it's tricky to track down the original author, it's a saying I grew up hearing regularly.

there is – proof a little change in daily habits can lead to drastic changes. How can we live out our best day if we don't know where we're going? Now I'm fired up and ranting, sounding all preachy and shit.

Before we continue, I want to share with you a thought-provoking declaration: we must know who we have to become, to get to where we want to go. Developing healthy habits helps massively with this cause. Applicable daily habits make it even easier to accomplish. That's why at the end of each section in this book you'll find an action plan to help you put each habit into place.

THE RESET EQUATION

What's the most important part of life? Time. No matter your financial status or how influential you are, time is the single greatest commodity known to humankind. Once it's gone, it's gone. Why then do so many of us continuously waste it? Time is everything. Consistency is key and positive momentum are all major players in our healthy habit reset equation.

How much time do you think it takes to create new and healthy daily habits? How long do you think it takes to break these habits once you develop them? Those are two questions with two very different answers that may surprise you. Let's talk about creating new patterns of behaviour first. There are multiple credible studies out there that have put a specific time frame[5]. The numbers 66 are what the experts seem to have landed on[6].

---

5   Lally, P., van Jaarsveld, C. H., Potts, H. W., & Wardle, J. (2010).
6   How are habits formed: Modelling habit formation in the real world. European Journal of Social Psychology, 40(6), 998-1009.

Basically, two months. This seems a bit too specific for my liking, how about you?

Looking back at my life, I know I've put myself in some toxic situations derived from poor daily choices and those outcomes surely didn't take 66 days to get there, they seemed to have occurred overnight. To be fair, the scientific studies mentioned above (see footnotes) focus on repetition. In other words, the positive side of habits, not the toxic version that my mind immediately wanders to. It's important to also mention that consistency and repetition are key to developing a healthy new pattern of behaviour. The idea is to stick with it long enough in that it becomes automatic. This is why goal setting, journalling and positive reinforcement all help reinforce and increase the likelihood of success.

On the other hand, from a fitness perspective, it seems unfair how quickly we lose results we've worked so hard to achieve. Have you ever challenged yourself to get into decent cardio shape? If you have, then you know how hard it is to progress and at the same time you also know how quickly you lose your results if you get lazy. It's tough to find accurate science on this but it's one of the major variables that deter people who have been in shape in the past but the hill seems too steep to climb again so they never give it another crack.

Back to the 66 days, once you start learning and developing these habits for yourself you may find that time frame differs for you personally. 66 days? 21 days? 254 days? Relax, I'm not teaching these timeframes in this book. These methods only take 24 hours.

How can this possibly be true, you ask? Easy. It comes down to perspective. We all know it's important to plan and create long term goals ourselves but depending on where you're positioned at in your life, the long term view can be daunting. Simplifying this perspective is ideal. In life, nothing is ever guaranteed. Focusing on the present moment will assist you with managing stress. This awareness will help with accomplishing your daily goals along with maintaining a simplistic approach. Repeat. Reset. ISD1MF: It's Still Day 1 Motherf#$ker.

WHAT DOES IT MEAN TO PRESS RESET?

Reset: VERB: to set again or anew, to change the reading of often to zero.

> '... suffering has been stronger than all other teaching and has taught me to understand what your heart used to be. I have been bent and broken but—I hope— into a better shape.'
> — Charles Dickens

HINDSIGHT 2020

We can all agree 2020 was a reset for the world. Seemingly overnight, learning how to pivot became more important than any daily task. Companies, families, businesses, and organisations all needed to re-evaluate the way they've always done things.

I thought to myself, *What about the individual though? What about us?*

What once was, 'How It's Done,' suddenly turned into, 'Is this really necessary for us to be productive?' and 'Do we really need to go to the office every day to be successful?'

I've always been one to find the silver lining during adverse moments, but things seemed different this time. With the COVID-19 pandemic and the global disarray it caused, I was forced to examine my own existence a bit closer. I was forced to sit alone with myself for many hours, going over my existence like an old school flicker book, attempting to fine-tune things that had gone wrong.

The last six or so years, have been the best years of my life. I've started various successful businesses; I've become a published author, and my personal relationships have never been more enriched. With all this being said, the truth was loud and clear; my daily flaws were starting to add up and I knew there were many areas of my life that needed to be improved…

I've pondered many questions over the last twelve months relating to my own mortality. By no means am I saying I'm grateful for the panic, heartbreak, and chaos 2020 brought to the world, all I'm saying is I'm fortunate for the time spent alone, hidden away in introspective thought.

In the years that followed, many of the same questions kept arising in my head: *Am I wasting my days doing things that no longer serve me?*

What habits have I held onto that no longer speak to my spirit, my true self? How many moments am I taking for granted? Do I honestly appreciate the little things? Am I living my most optimised life?

As I wrestled with these questions, it wasn't stress or anxiety I felt, but more along the lines of inspiration. I became inspired by the chaos and noise of the world. I immediately started writing and brainstorming ways I could do things differently. As I gave these thoughts more attention, areas in my life that I could drastically improve upon suddenly started popping up everywhere. Yes, I was already living an active and healthy lifestyle but I knew I could give more.

Like my father would always say, 'Jonny, you're half-assing it.' I was being lazy. These thought-provoking conversations sparked my willingness to share with you what exactly I had come up with. I was fine-tuning the small things. I was sharpening the tools that had been a bit worn down.

ACTION PLAN

Use the following eight habits as a tool for your mental and physical health. Experiment with them. When learning about certain time frames of either sleeping or eating, do what makes you feel comfortable. Remember, nothing is ever in stone.

My life was once filled with frustration, bitterness and stress. I've started over many times before. I've pressed reset many times before. I've taught myself it's never too late to become what you were always meant to be.

CHAPTER ONE

HABIT ONE: FORGET THE SNOOZE

WHAT IS PERSPECTIVE?

Perspective: NOUN: a particular attitude towards or way of thinking or regarding something; a point of view.

'If you stop looking for a shortcut...and find your discipline and your will then you will find your freedom.[7]'
— Jocko Willink

The only thing I disagree with about the above quote is the word "find". I don't believe that we as humans should be relying on the fact we are left to haplessly, 'find our way' or 'find our discipline' but I'm using the quote anyway, because it's powerful and it's aligned with my message (I can be quite bitchy, even in compliments, so let's switch out "find" for create and focus on the overall intent of Willink).

I was watching the evening news when I first learned about Jocko Willink. It was an old clip of him being questioned by the courts regarding a military issue. His behaviour was unusually responsive. By responsive, I mean accountable. He wasn't making

---
7 Willink, 2017, p. 56.

excuses for the actions of his team but taking ownership. To understand this event, I must quickly give you some context.

Jocko is as a man who believes in personal growth and accountability. The news clip ended with a video description of Jocko telling a story about an interaction he recently had between himself and a military colleague.

The energy of his message was solely based around two different, yet very normal, human mindsets. One is the perspective of opportunity, and the other is the perspective of consequence. It's how we think and act during situations presented to us where much stress and dismay are present. He presented the audience with a story where two characters are presented with the same situation but individually they choose to handle adversity very differently.

One example he used was a missed job opportunity, character one succumbed to the pressure. He was defeated from the rejection and allowed it to consume his entire being. He brought the failure with him everywhere he turned, from his workplace to his home and the moment consumed him. He became a victim of the consequences of his attitude. Character two on the other hand, who experienced the exact same situation was not deterred by the rejection. He looked at it as an opportunity to grow, he told himself, 'Good. So, what if I didn't get the job that I so longed for? I now have more time to get better.'

What a wild thought, right? To experience a bummer and be motivated from it. Character two perceived the setback as a simple part of the course, he chose to learn rather than grieve. It's a powerful mindset to have, you can align this way of thinking throughout your life and use it when something bad happens to you. We're either a victim or we're not, we either live lives by choice or by consequence. Even as I'm rereading this it still hits me with goosebumps and excitement. Our perspectives shape and mould our reality. Our reality begins with each waking breath combined with the dawn or better known to you as… your alarm clock.

In this chapter I am going to talk about the importance of healthy habits, what they are, and how to create them, offering you a system you can adopt from the time you wake up in the morning until you go to bed to ensure you're living your most optimised twenty-four hours, every single day of your life. Healthy habits are everything we do that comprise our daily life, whether we have kids or not, whether we have roommates, whether we live with family or live on our own. Every little decision we make from the time our alarm goes off equates to how happy, healthy, and successful that day is going to be.

Something I talk about all the time with my clients is the role that the ring from the morning alarm clock has on our daily output. What we do and how we think from the time the alarm goes off, is a reflection of our mental framework. I challenge you to try this: rather than placing your phone near your bedside as most people do, find a different location. This will force you to get out of bed when the alarm goes off, enabling you to stay up rather than rolling over and complacently hitting snooze.

Never use it again. And I mean *never* hit the snooze button again.

I apologise if I'm sounding militant with this one, but it's been highly beneficial for me and here's why: hitting the snooze button tells yourself that you do not want to be up. It tells yourself you do not want to be there. The action of hitting the snooze, which in this case is your very first habit in the morning, is an extremely unhealthy one.

You just woke up, why are you starting your day with such an easy bad habit to fix? It's not a healthy process that any successful and happy person engages in. When that alarm goes off, you go off, you get up. How does an extra fifteen minutes of sleep *really* serve you? Physically, it serves no purpose, but mentally, not getting up can be quite detrimental.

My dad used to tell me a story about a lion and the antelope. On a biological and cellular level, the lion and the antelope are the same. The same? You ask. Yes. Pretty much, so, both are land animals, both breathe in oxygen, and both expel out carbon dioxide. Did you also know the lion never attacks the antelope face-to-face? The lion will only attack when the antelope turns and runs. When the antelope turns and runs, it becomes the prey, and the lion becomes the predator.

The running antelope is telling the lion it doesn't want to be there, so the lion attacks. In this case, be the lion when you're the antelope. Get it? In relation to the snooze button, if you hit the snooze, you're becoming the prey, not the predator, for your day. You're telling yourself you don't want to be there. Mentally, you're weakening your chances for achieving a strong and positive day. Let's test this. Real quick, add up how many days you press the snooze button, now equate that to weeks then months then years.

That's a whole lot of lying around, right?

A simple adjustment and easy habit change from hitting the snooze button to not hitting it can lead to many improvements in your life. How will you know? Try it out tomorrow, then again on the next day. It's wise to never undervalue the power of the mundane and "easy" habits in relation to drastic life improvements. Everything you need to accomplish and to achieve your most optimal day, whether it's Monday, whether it's Thursday, whether it's Sunday, happens before you even leave your bedroom. There are certain victories that present themselves as soon as we wake up.

When we look at life, we view it in a step-by-step format, this is what I call the 'momentum scale'. Think about it this way; when bad things happen, they usually happen in sequences. On the contrary, when good things happen, they also happen in sequences, is this just coincidence? I don't think so.

My point is: be aware of these moments, once we are aware we then can create systems within our daily habits to either negate the bad momentum or promote the positive. This is called momentum. We have the opportunity when we wake up to create either positive or negative momentum and the way we do this is through our choices and actions before we even leave the bedroom. Attitude is everything. The way we approach any task will directly affect the quality of the outcome. Our mind is a powerful tool filled with malleable reasoning skills. This isn't calculus or physics, the simplicity in the action of you waking up with the alarm rather than hitting the snooze, can make this habit seem ordinary or basic. Remember, every great invention starts with one simple action. The morning is no different, it's your choice how you want to attack it.

INTERVIEW HIGHLIGHTS FROM WELLNESS EXPERT, AUBREY MARCUS

I first became aware of Aubrey Marcus by listening to his podcast back in 2015. He's a guy who commands attention when he speaks and is also a very good storyteller, both are traits I admire. He's great at business, health and wellness and communicates his views extremely intellectually. Aubrey lives in Austin, Texas and is an experimentalist, unconventional fitness enthusiast, and human optimiser. He is the CEO of Onnit, an optimal human performance company he's built into one of the fastest growing companies in America. Aubrey's personal and professional mission rests on a single question: How can we get the most out of our bodies, minds, and systems, on a daily basis? His ability to answer that question has drawn dozens of elite performers, hundreds of thousands of customers, and millions of fans to his company, Onnit.

In 2016 on my own podcast tour for my first show, I was fortunate enough to travel from Sydney to Austin, Texas and have a tour of his human performance centre "Onnit" and use the training facility. For a time my podcast, The Vision Board, was sponsored by Onnit and with that I became a student of Aubrey's. The following conversation between myself and Aubrey took place on June 11th, 2018, when Aubrey was a guest on my podcast *Ungoogleable*:

My Question: Where did this passion come from with your willingness to question things and learn to reach your full potential? Was this always in you since you were a young boy or is this something that has evolved because of certain scenarios in your life or were you influenced by someone or something?

Aubrey's Answer: I think it was a little bit of both, you know, I think for me as a kid I was someone who nobody that no adult figure could tell me to do this because 'I told you so'. I would not accept that answer. I'd be like, 'Why?' I need to understand it. If I understood it, then I would go along with it.

My parents raised me in kind of a very libertarian philosophy, where they wanted me to understand the consequences of my choices and I think that's a mistake that a lot of parents make is that they treat children like little idiots. Like, you can't even actually be an idiot. It's just that their brains haven't fully developed yet. They're a fully sentient being in development and I think my parents treating me like that and asking me to question things and even if there were issues to discuss at the dinner table like relationship issues with friends and things like that.

They would ask my opinion and get my brain working. I was basically trained to think philosophically about problems we were trying to solve in my own life and others, so, I think that was in me and cultivated by my parents.

My Question: I'm really intrigued by the philosophy called 'The Law of Subtraction,' the idea in life that less is more. We don't need to add things into our existence to make us more fulfilled, it's more about letting go of things or bad habits to create happiness, not adding more things in. Is there anything in your life recently that you've let go of that has enabled you to grow even more?

Aubrey's Answer: The biggest thing to let go of is your identity; your attachment to your identity. The emptier you can get, now this is getting more philosophical and metaphysical, but for me, the less attached you are to this persona this idea of whom you are—which gets harder the more well-known you become or the more your own personal brand gets out there—if you get attached to that, then you're always in the position of needing to defend it. And when you're needing to defend it, the body and mind treats it like its life or death and you're constantly stressed out. For me, letting go of my attachment to identity is one of the most challenging yet rewarding things that I'm really looking to do. It's about internal processes, it's never about the external things. It's about getting the insides right and letting the outside world fall into place from that.

My Question: A lot of my clients ask many questions on the physical aspect of training the body but in my opinion what's equally, if not more important, is the recovery side of things; how we can reduce stress, learning and practising the benefits of meditation. I know you're a proponent of recovery and mediation, can you explain a little bit more about why everyone should be doing it?

Aubrey's Answer: Firstly, I do have a meditation course that's part of my personal journey that I share with willing participants. You can find it on my website at www.aubreymarcus.com. It's a system that includes guided mediations to help people grow from a novice to an advanced meditation practitioner in a pretty short period of time. Meditation is absolutely one of the most vital things we can do, to adequately chart your course anywhere. First you have to get still. I mean, you can't even see the horizon when your emotions are high and your mind is running a million miles an hour, you're checking your phone every two minutes. How are you supposed to envision where you want to go in life until you can get still? Meditation is one of the great ways to get still.

Follow Aubrey on all social media channels @aubreymarcus and check his company out at www.onnit.com

INTERVIEW HIGHLIGHTS FROM WELLNESS EXPERT, GABBY REECE

My personal interests on progress and personal development became the basis of my first book. I researched specific habits of successful people along with various elements of human potential such as mindset and preparation. I interviewed many highflyers for that book and one of them was legendary big wave surfer Laird Hamilton. Laird's wife of many years just happens to be famous athlete, model, TV show host, and entrepreneur Gabby Reece.

As a boy I used to watch Gabby on TV dominate the beach volleyball scene and I always likened her to the female version of Karch Kiraly, a childhood hero of mine, who just happens to be the greatest volleyball player to have ever lived, well, at least to my twelve-year-old self.

I knew I wanted to chat with Gabby so through the network of podcasting, I was able to sit down with her and ask her a few questions that pertained to progress and health and learn from her. The following conversation between myself and Gabby Reece took place on June 15th, 2020, whilst Gabby was a guest on my podcast *Ungoogleable*:

My Question: I was recently listening to one of your podcasts and you were talking about "The Pursuit." This lifelong pursuit that we all have when we have goals; when we want to achieve something, when we want to grow and get to a certain place, and it's almost like it never feels good enough for us individually. Somebody like yourself, your resume is unbelievable, anybody can search your name and find out for themselves, can you talk about how you deal with your own pursuit and maybe some advice for people out there who feel that they're just not enough or maybe they feel inadequate even though they're giving it their all?

Gabby's Answer: You know, it's an interesting thought because I must be honest, a lot of what I have and the things that are behind me that are now sort of officially on paper that are considered part of my body of work were all just me living out questions of curiosities. Listen, not in an uncalculated sort of way,

I think it's sort of lining up who you are and where you think you're moving towards and then as things arise, you go, 'Hey, does this feel good or not?', 'Should I work really hard at this?', 'What if this never works out?', 'Will I still be ahead, just having tried?' I think even from very young, I naturally had things that would guide me through that process of wondering if something was worth pursuing.

So, let's say if someone is listening and they're feeling that they're not doing enough, I think you must first ask yourself, 'Why?' And that really comes back to our value systems and our individual definition of what success is. The world gives us a basket of definitions about what success is and I actually think that real success starts first with your definition.

Let's say you're feeling inadequate. That could also be that you're not satisfied with the types of relationships or the depths of relationships that you're having. Maybe your lifestyle choices are knowingly flawed, how's your diet? Are you moving your body? It's never just one feeling within a professional pursuit or passion but also looking at life, one's personal life; it all adds up.

My Question: [This question is about Gabby's human performance company, XPT] I wish more people understood the value and potential of breath work, you know, diaphragmatic breathing to reduce pain. I know that you practice and teach multiple natural disciplines regarding healing the body of pain and fatigue. When you're combining these healthy habits, what are your intentions as you're offering these practises out into the world? As the breath work and the movement are all connected, what was your inspiration behind all that?

Gabby's Answer: Honestly, going back to breath if you think about it, breath is the essence of life and most of us are doing it wrong including me. Many times throughout the day I catch myself, 'Oh, nice chest breathing'. A friend of ours, Rick Rubin, years ago, introduced Laird to Wim Hoff. When you get into breath, it's really one of the oldest practises, it's sort of like saying "bone broth", people are like, 'Uh, okay, you know, really?'

So, then we then started to really figure out how to incorporate it into our daily lives, we created an overall practise. I think if you're an athlete or not, you train a long time or when I say "athlete" I mean someone who's using their body for work. You start to go, Breathe, Move, Recover, those are the fundamentals for XPT.

Breathing? If we're not doing that right then we're not helping ourselves out in one of the easiest ways that we can. Moving, as animals we should be moving but then the idea of recovery, active recovery or anticipating your recovery, do heat and ice and certain modalities where I can accelerate and support my recovery so I can train harder, I can keep inflammation down, age in the most vital way that I can. What happened was that we simply decided to put all these things together, it's kind of just what we were always doing.

You must realise too, there are always things that are going to be more important. We know its healthier to get to bed sooner than later, being hydrated is going to be important, avoiding certain foods are always going to be important but the hope with XPT is using what we've been learning.

We are students, we don't really know anything actually and we'll give you the best we know right now and then if you see us in six months or two years and say, 'That was working, and we found that this is working better', so at least there's some flexibility. I think it's important to never speak in intense absolutes about, 'You have to do it this way, because this is the only way'. I think we are all really different, I think there's seasons, there's times of our lives where some of us are highly stressed, maybe they shouldn't be banging much iron, maybe they should be doing more breathing and nurturing their systems, this is one of our main messages.

HABIT ONE: ACTION PLAN

Keeping structure throughout the week is the secret to success for many high-flying individuals. Ensuring your energy systems are primed for optimal output is key. Set your alarm for the same wake up time every day, weekends included. Work on regimenting a consistent sleep pattern as well. This will enable your body to stay in a regulated state allowing it to never get confused or shocked by twisted routines. Patterns that are consistently repeated, are extremely important in relation to maintaining healthy habits.

The point is: choose a time to wake up and stick with it, even on weekends and holidays. Your body is a machine. It requires rhythm and balance to run efficiently.

Create an easy to achieve 'Mental Prep' checklist. This will assist you with counter balancing the urge to press the snooze, especially on mornings when you're feeling a bit run down. This task should consist of a few quick little 'to dos' that you can execute directly after you shut your alarm off. This might include things like: setting gratitude for the day, and taking a few long deep breaths. Doing this the moment, you wake up will enable you to positively kick start your mind and body in preparation for the day.

Most importantly, rise out of bed with purpose. Having a sense of accomplishment is vital for your mental health. Don't judge yourself on your failures, acknowledge them, make the proper adjustments and move forward. Focus on your successes.

Sadly, most people never focus on the so-called mundane tasks that are executed day in and day out, yet it's these tasks that promote a positive mindset along with a successful and healthy lifestyle. The smallest victories are equally as important as the biggest ones but only if you allow them to be. On that note I must ask you, have you made your bed today?

CHAPTER TWO

HABIT TWO: MAKE YOUR BED

WHAT IS DISCIPLINE

Discipline: NOUN: the practice of training people to obey rules or a code of behaviour, using forms punishment to correct disobedience. It can also be a branch of knowledge, typically studied in higher education.

'If you make your bed every morning you will have accomplished the first task of the day. It will give you a small sense of pride and it will encourage you to do another task and another and another... and, if by chance you have a miserable day, you will come home to a bed that is made, and a made bed gives you encouragement that tomorrow will be better.'
— William McRaven

No disrespect to Admiral McRaven but I didn't learn this philosophy from him. My father is the one who taught me this as a young boy. He would talk about the importance of controlling what we can control, no matter the situation we're faced with in life, and how this plays a vital role in self-worth. The idea that we showcase discipline when no one is watching is just as important as when everyone is watching. He'd say, 'act as if' and I knew what he meant.

My father wasn't a military man, but he was wise and philosophical and finding out about a high-ranking military official using a similar philosophy to my dad made me happy and astonished to say the least. Old Bill, has notoriety so it's only fitting I reference him here. (I must disagree with him on a point though: making the bed isn't the first accomplished task of the day. By this step, we've already beat the snooze, so making the bed will be our second small victory).

The admiral gave this exceptional speech at the University of Texas, Austin, in which he forever immortalised himself with a charismatic delivery but very simple message. I'm not sure if you guys have ever spent time around a military man but if you have, you'd agree with me when I say that they're generally very colourful storytellers. One of my favourite things about visiting my hometown to see my family is when my brother-in-law Ed picks me up from the airport. He's a Chief in the Air Force and from the moment the tires hit the road and leave the terminal up until we pull into his house a little over an hour away, I'm gifted multiple detailed stories about secret missions, foreign lands and the odd conspiracy. So, when I read the admiral's speech I wasn't surprised, I kind of expected it. That doesn't take away how remarkable his message is.

Admiral McRaven tells a story about his career in the military and how he progressed through to join an elite special forces group. He gives examples of heroism, selflessness and sacrifice. He talks about the darkest of moments in which he learned to never take life for granted and he shares some beautiful stories of how exceptional and brave the human spirit can be when faced with dire circumstances.

Ten minutes in, and the room is captivated by this war hero, he's sharing statistics about the brutality of war and the contrast of life and death. For a moment you feel as if he's either giving a eulogy or an Oscar's speech but then just as any great storyteller always does, he grabs you with: 'And Here's My Top 10 Things I Learned as a Navy Seal'. The astounding fact wasn't his list, or him being a Seal, but his reasoning for why his men were always successful and safe once their mission was up.

He states, 'It's because we made our bed.' He mentions that if you want to change the world for the better than start with small little tasks, tiny minuscule actions that are achievable on a daily basis. As he finishes, he repeats, 'So if you want to change the world, then start by making your bed.'

Wild right? Advice from a war hero, not to run a mile, not to learn a martial art, not to act out but to take action at the simplest of levels starting within your own bedroom.

I must admit, the message I was given from my father never had the concise worldly advice about changing the world but I can tell you the habit is deeply engrained in my daily mechanics, which in turn enables me to be the best coach I can be, which then helps my clients. This is another mundane task that seems to be influential in successful people's lives.

Have you made your bed today? It's all good if you didn't, you'll start tomorrow. It's interesting to learn different perspectives people have on this bed-making topic. I find it's usually a generational thing. My dad was an outcome of immigrant parents who preached respect and discipline. Admiral McRaven is a military man who values the code of honour and ethics. I like to view the world in more of a Utopian philosophy. Not the societal utopia you're thinking of but more of a personal and mentally positive utopia.

It's why I call the aforementioned make your bed habit, the "Burning Man" philosophy.

For those of you who are unfamiliar with the social gathering festival in the middle of the desert in the United States called, 'Burning Man', whatever your opinion on this event is here's one fact about it at least from my experience, the participants and festival revellers leave the space/land they use exactly how it was when they got there, if not better.

From what I've heard and experienced, that's why it's called 'Burning Man' because on the last day, the congregation meets in this area they call 'the playa' and they have this huge celebration. One last hoorah to commemorate their experiences. They build this huge structure from their belongings and take everything, all their objects, everything that they brought, and they burn it. They have a festival of dance and song and it's an amazing moment around a fire, this mountain of fiery joy, this pile of things they once possessed but now ceases to exist.

Why? Because days earlier they found the space/land empty and vast and the idea is to leave the property exactly how they found it, or better. This is the principle I use every morning. No matter how shitty the day before went, you go to work, you go to your job, maybe even need to go to the doctor, you receive bad news; it's life. Shit happens.

Whatever it may be, when you come back at night and you come into your bedroom, you get changed and your bed is made. You left your space just as you found it, sometimes you have left it even better. This is not only a physical benefit to your space, but it serves your mental health as well. It is emotionally and psychologically beneficial too. Visually, you are seeing something you've taken care of. Your space is not in shambles, so if anything, the habit of making your bed for the visual learner is a huge mental victory.

Now, one other thing I suggest you do before you leave your bedroom is to take a deep breath, focus on yourself, set intentions for your day. Don't grab your phone, don't grab your laptop, don't check what the morning's breaking news is, don't even send that text to your loved ones.

Before you do all that stuff, sit with yourself at the edge of your bed and take a few deep breaths. Inhale through the nose exhale through the mouth. Let's do it again. In through the nose and exhale through the mouth. Remember, when we breathe in through the nose our stomach should go out and when we breathe out of the mouth our stomach should go in. Take five deep breaths, inhales and exhales and set your intentions for the day. Tell yourself in these breaths what you are going to do, what you want to do.

Lastly, probably the most important thing, set gratitude for the day because you just woke up. Tell yourself you are grateful for being here; you are grateful for breathing; you are grateful for being alive and you are grateful for this day and you want to be here. Our mindset and perspective are a direct outcome of our habits.

How you do something is how you do everything. Playing the victim when things go wrong is the easiest role to engage in, but what if you reversed it?

What would the results be if you started practising positive mental behaviours instead of negative ones? Would your life change much if you started viewing your reality with a similar perspective? How much would you accomplish if you conditioned yourself to focus on only the good things rather than the bad things? Be your best friend, it shouldn't feel weird to cheer for yourself. Love yourself, it's a simple message to tell yourself and don't be afraid to give yourself credit for all the little things that you accomplish.

INTERVIEW HIGHLIGHTS FROM HUMAN BEHAVIOURAL SPECIALIST, DR JOHN DEMARTINI

I'm not sure if you believe in fate or happenstance, but the story about how I managed an in person sit down interview with Dr John Demartini is unique. At the time, I was co-hosting a podcast in Sydney and hadn't yet done an entire interview on my own. I was going through my normal routine sending messages and emails to potential guests trying to book them in for future podcasts. I'd sent an invite to Dr John Demartini, an expert in life mastery and the Law of Attraction. He's been featured in both the hit movie and bestselling book titled *The Secret*. He's also a very successful entrepreneur, teacher and businessman.

To my shock, I received an immediate reply to my email. Organising interviews, agreeing on a date and time for all parties involved normally takes a few weeks, but this time was different. Even more thrilling than John's immediate response to my message was his willingness to do the show. He just happened to be arriving in Sydney that day on his boat and was doing a seminar at a very illustrious hotel that coming weekend.

I was in a pickle. Not only didn't I have my co-host with me, I had also impulsively said yes to the podcast interview request without thinking about the prep required to pull something like this off. I had put myself in a sink or swim scenario. My prep work generally consists of at least a week's worth of planning for each guest but John only had time for tomorrow so I had to make it work.

The following conversation between myself and Dr John Demartini took place on February 12th, 2018, while John was a guest on my podcast *Ungoogleable*:

My Question: [This question is based around John's mastery programs that promote and teach self-discipline] How would you describe 'life mastery' and what advice would you give to those people who are interested in bettering themselves?

John's Answer: I've been teaching Life Mastery for over twenty-five years. I've had all different ages there, sometimes I have parents that run companies and have their children come see me. Normally teens and twenty somethings, or entrepreneurs who want to go into something to improve their life. [Life Mastery is] a philosophy on what exactly are your priorities in life, what do you want to accomplish in life. It can be business, it can be financial, it can be educational, it can be social, it can be family related; it can be physical health related. Anything that can help them master their life.

What I've done is compiled around two thousand questions, so it's like me standing over their shoulder like a consultant, helping them answer questions about what they really want and how they're going to get it. Basically, [it's] sitting for three days and executively planning. Then I will float around, or my assistants will float around and do whatever we can to assist people in clarifying that. Then, when they're done, they'll print out a booklet which will be about 250 pages just exactly how they want their life; what they want to accomplish and when they want to accomplish it. It can be updated and refined anytime they see fit.

It's extremely important to write out what you want to achieve in life then equally as important is the planning and discipline that comes along with it.

My Question: Some people are under the impression that there is no individual ceiling for one's full potential. Maybe it's the decisions that we make or the momentum we create that either depicts where we are in life or where we are going. Have you ever felt [there was a time] in your life that you weren't going to live up to your full potential?

John's Answer: I don't think that any human being can live up to their full potential. I think that that's a little bit of a delusion because the second you achieve something, you see possibilities in achieving something greater. I think we all have goals; we're all shooting for stars and maybe the Moon kind of thing.

'Full Potential' I don't know that there's any human being that reaches their full potential. We reach ever greater degrees of potential as we learn how to refine our behaviour and master our lives and learn new skills and surround ourselves with more empowering people, those things, but I don't think there's an end to it. I don't think that anybody ever… is "done" or it's reached. I think it's an approximation to ever greater degrees.

One last thing about Dr Demartini, if you're familiar with the Law of Attraction or the idea that one can create a positive life be sure to look him up. He was featured in the book and film called *The Secret* all about asking the universe for the things you desire. Remember when I told you it was a unique story?

INTERVIEW HIGHLIGHTS FROM RETIRED UFC FIGHTER AND UNITED STATES ARMY RANGER, TIM KENNEDY

As a lifelong athlete and student of progress, I've always been drawn towards people who've done or are doing great things that are driven by practice and discipline. It's no secret I'm a fan of martial arts and combat sports. I can list almost every UFC event since its infancy in 1993.

That being said, it's not very often in any sport that you see an athlete at the highest level competing against the best athletes in the world while simultaneously serving their country. For me it was quite profound watching Tim Kennedy fight in both Strikeforce and then the UFC against the best fighters in the world. Then I learned that he was also a veteran/active-duty serviceman. I knew I wanted to pick his brain on a few things, and lucky for me my relationship with Onnit enabled me to reaching out to Tim's camp which eventually resulted our sit down.

The following conversation between myself and US Army Ranger, special forces sniper and retired UFC fighter, Tim Kennedy took place on May 23rd, 2018, while Tim was a guest on my podcast *Ungoogleable*:

My Question: What is the feeling like when you're in the second round or the third round of a fight and you know that your body is telling you to quit but your spirit is telling you to fight? What's that psychological battle like?

Tim's Answer: It's hell. It is absolute torture. My brain knows what is supposed to happen but it feels like you're in sand. You're moving in mud, like you're trying to punch in water and it's like, I know I'm supposed to move my feet but they're not moving how they're supposed to move. It's like I'm too tough for my own good, where it's like, I know I should quit.

One of my fights, I horrifically tore my hamstring in the first round during the last take down which took place in the first minute. From that point on, I couldn't move my leg. Then the conditioning caught up with the torn hamstring and it just got…

it was like an existential moment where you're having an out of body experience watching yourself take part in a fight and you're like, 'Oh my God, there's a really, really, really bad version of what I'm supposed to be capable of,' and then you are kind of embarrassed. Like: Why did I do that, that's not what I'm supposed to do, oh my God, what am I doing now? That's not what I'm supposed to do either. That wasn't part of the gameplan. Then it just gets really depressing and sad and pathetic and humiliating. It's the discipline though that enables me to push through those dark times.

My Question: You have such conviction, persistence, drive, motivation, what is the origin of all that? Is that something that's always been with you? What is the light that's fuelling that fire?

Tim's Answer: I think I've always been this way. It's developed. I've gotten more passionate about it. If at this point, I wasn't part of something bigger than myself and I wasn't contributing to something that was more meaningful than just who I am, then everything that I've done, for the people I've killed, and the villages that have been burnt; it would be for nothing. It would be maddening. It would drive me insane.

I'd be a crazy person if I looked back and I was like, 'Oh my God, I have done all of these things for myself, or because I enjoyed it.' Or any other horrible and horrific realisation, besides helping people or because it's just the right thing to do. It's part of the greater good. It's because I believe in freedom, that a girl should be able to go to school and not have acid thrown in her face. You shouldn't be able to beat or force people to work in your opium fields so you can then sell it to Pakistan.

If I wasn't positively contributing to humanity and mankind, then I'd be insane. I'd be an undisciplined crazy person.

HABIT TWO: ACTION PLAN

Your mind is wired to see the world in two categories: things you accomplish versus things you've yet to accomplish. Because of this, it's imperative that you have systems within your day to adhere to. Organising, prioritising and achieving simple tasks positively benefits your mental landscape as well as helps to boost your internal drive.

Making your bed might not sound like a big deal but it is, it's all part of a greater equation of accomplishments. The first twenty minutes of your mornings need to be littered with easy, yet attainable, goals. Creating a routine and sticking to it will only elevate your mood and increase your focus over long periods of time. Here's a few pro tips from me to you that'll help with your daily framework.

My Early Systems: after I shut my alarm off and make my bed, I'll mentally go over what I'm grateful for that day. My family and my health are always atop the list. I will then create a short two-minute breathing exercise that involves deep inhalations with a short breath hold combined with bigger exhalations with another minor breath hold. If patterned breath work is foreign to you, simply search the internet for Boxed Breathing Examples. Everything from making sure my coffee filter is cleaned to filling up my filtered water jug in my fridge, the way I handle my morning routine is a reflection on how I handle my entire day.

Remember, accomplishment is vital for maintaining a healthy and positive mind, the trick is to create patterns throughout your day that put you in a position in which you're constantly achieving and consistently improving on things. Speaking on improvement and achievement, have you eaten today? Should you? Eat I mean, it's a necessity, right? All the time? All day? Well, is it?

CHAPTER THREE

HABIT THREE: F$%K BREAKFAST

WHAT IS INTUITION?

Intuition: NOUN: The ability to understand something instinctively, without the need for conscious reasoning.

'The clash between science and religion has not shown that religion is false, and science is true. It has shown that all systems of definition are relative to various purposes, and that none of them grasp reality.'
— Alan Watts

I'm laughing out loud, thinking about how many readers are reading this now and thinking to yourself, *Why is there a definition about intuition and a quote about science and religion under the chapter about breakfast?* But the fields I work in are as dogmatic as cults and religious groups. It's as divisive as politics, and as petty as fourth grade lunchrooms, especially when the word "Nutrition" is mentioned. They say fortune favours the brave and in this case the bravery comes in the form of words.

When I stumbled upon Alan Watts in 2013, I was immediately captivated. An Englishman who trained in Buddhism just seemed out of place to me at the time. He would go on to author and co-author books on eastern and western religion. The more I learned about him the more I became intrigued. Maybe it was his fascination with consciousness that interested me, or the idea that a man could spend his entire life researching, studying and testing something that is impossible to touch. I guess that's any belief though—when we wholeheartedly subscribe to any idea, we forgo the conclusion of fact on the basis of faith, even if it's blind.

To say I was late to the party in appreciating Watts is an understatement, but then again, I've always been a late bloomer. I had just moved to Australia from Las Vegas with a brand-new Masters of Leadership and Personal Development. My paperwork and credentials were starting to match my thought processes, but my day job at the time, or should I say night job, was still lacking. I was paying the bills by late night drinking and bartending.

I used to visit YouTube and search the site for videos on inspiration and motivation. You know, featuring the sort of cheesy guy who talks a big game but falls short on the playing field type of thing. I wasn't short on confidence or drive; it was perspective I was lacking. On one of these random searches, I serendipitously found an Alan Watts video. In the video he was talking about intuition, the meaning of life, and many other conscious expanding ideas. His words were:

> *But my dear man, reality is only a Rorschach inkblot, you know.*[8]

I had to sit with these words for a while. At the time I couldn't fully grasp the idea that individual perception played such a key role in one's happiness. I thought we all were playing the same game with the same guidelines.

---

8 Watts, 1951, p. 52.

> *We do not "come into" this world; we come out of it, as leaves from a tree. As the ocean "waves," the universe "peoples." Every individual is an expression of the whole realm of nature, a unique action of the total universe[9].*

In this moment, I crumbled. Instantly, I knew where I'd been going wrong in life. I was waiting for someone to help me while believing I deserve better. I was a victim to my own thoughts. To my ego, it was a cruel realisation but for my future self it was ever so important that I computed those words.

> *And people get all fouled up because they want the world to have meaning as if it were words... As if you had a meaning, as if you were a mere word, as if you were something that could be looked up in a dictionary. You are meaning.[10]*

All this time I thought my life was static, that I was the victim of my circumstances, but the harsh reality was that my own choices led me to think that way. I expected a different outcome but I was not putting in the effort.

> *We feel that our actions are voluntary when they follow a decision and involuntary when they happen without decision. But if a decision itself were voluntary every decision would have to be preceded by a decision to decide – An infinite regression which fortunately does not occur. Oddly enough, if we had to decide to decide, we would not be free to decide.*

How many times did you have to reread that? Don't lie. It's pretty wordy, but old Alan was right. My interpretation is that it's wise for us to never compartmentalise our wins and losses. Don't celebrate wins too long, yet let's not make excuses for our faults to protect our emotions. They're one and the same. Our ego tells us

---

9   Watts, 1958, p. 17
10 Watts, 1951, p. 21

that we matter yet tricks us into believing that we don't, especially if it fits the narrative when we mess up.

After hours of being mesmerised by Watt's videos, I told myself, *Wow, you don't need to follow the standard lines of life to feel accomplished and free, you just have to help people.* I remember being at a coffee shop in Sydney, writing about my goal of wanting to help people.

It seems as if it were in the same moment that I started coaching and teaching the way of health and wellness. It wasn't; it took me a few years to get my coaching business off the ground, but when I did, I never looked back. Over time, Watts taught me the value of intuition. In my experience, most coaches will only learn and teach what they read, which limits them from thinking outside of the box in regards to their health, and their client's needs. Because of exposure to Watts and other great thinkers, I have never done things the way most fitness experts would advise. One of those things is my stance on breakfast.

Here we go. Ready? F@#K BREAKFAST! No, my bad.

What I *meant* was that if you want to get your day started off on the right foot, then DON'T BREAK YOUR FAST.

What should you eat for breakfast? Here's the juicy bit I promised, what I'm going to tell you next will be controversial. Here's what you should eat: NOTHING.

Let me tell you why.

When I wake up in the morning, I don't mentally frame or hold true actions and habits that were given to me by my parents or by my teachers as truths. I live and practise my habits through personal experiences with my body and through the results I have with my clients. A lot of our issues and problems as adults arise due to bad information we were given when we were children.

Life doesn't come with roadmaps or "how to" manuals. Our parents were just kids who had kids and so on and so forth. There's zero science that suggests one diet is better than the next. Not everyone is the same. Our genetics play a role, our geographical ancestry plays a role in relation to ideal nutritional habits. There's also zero evidence suggesting waking up in the morning and eating is healthy.

Food is tricky, we have to take into consideration traditions and culture, we have to be empathetic to socioeconomic variables. My point is this: just because someone told you something doesn't make it right. I must also state, just because this works for me doesn't mean it will work for you. If you're living with a medical condition, be sure to contact your doctor before making any sudden changes to your diet.

My stance has been informed by eight years of observational research with willing human participants (go now to view the nice colourful pictures in the back). I'm an active adult who doesn't drink alcohol or smoke cigarettes. I monitor my bodyweight composition per fat and muscle and I also measure my recovery based on sleep habits and heart rate (I'll get into the importance of sleep later on).

Based on my childhood in America, my opinion is that breakfast is one of the worst habits to start your day. Let's look at breakfast from a traditional western standpoint. Traditionally, it is going to be filled with a lot of processed carbohydrates, cereals, breads, toasts. All that stuff is going to be mixed with a lot of sugars, syrups, candied flavoured drinks and juices. It's also going to be filled with a lot of things called empty calories or low satiated foods, basically foods that will make you feel full initially, then they will make you feel like trash and then a few hours later you will be hungry again. This is the definition of low nutrient dense foods.

I say throw away breakfast. I haven't eaten breakfast in over five years and when I stopped eating breakfast, I started feeling better about myself. I started losing weight, I started losing that belly bloat and I started having more energy.

We go to sleep at night for eight hours, we are lying stationary, we wake up in the morning, we have not moved, we were just sleeping, and the first thing we do to our bodies is put food in it. It's truly a moronic concept, that idea suggests we need to eat. Our mindset around breakfast is why there are countless health issues with things such as heart disease, diabetes, obesity and countless other lifestyle related diseases.

Many of these can be avoided if we just cut down on the empty calories. Why would we start our day off with so much negative calories when we have so many positive things we need to accomplish?

But what about coffee or tea? Enjoy it. I do, but the last thing we want to do is to put our digestive system into overdrive. Look at your body as a machine or a computer. If that machine is on for countless hours and countless days without shutting it off or restarting it, things are going to act up. It's going to go haywire. It's the same thing for our small intestine, our digestive system. We need a reset.

Skipping breakfast, let us call that your "digestive reset". Initially, this could be a little tricky depending on your overall health at the time of reading this; how overweight and out of shape you are has an impact. But like anything else, the more time spent in the practice and the discipline, the better understanding you will have and the more you will get used to it.

More importantly, your hunger will fade.

It's a form of psychosis, thinking we need to be eating when we wake up. It's a pattern of behaviour given to us by people who had zero understanding about nutrition and the human body. The fact is, you don't need to eat breakfast. You just woke up, drink a tall glass of water and if you need an energy boost, make yourself a coffee.

At the end of the day, if you're fit and healthy keep doing what you're doing but if you're not, what do you have to lose? A few pounds or kilos?

Your instincts are woven within you to serve not to harm. Are you doing things on a daily basis that are positively serving you? The only way you can truly tap into your intuition and instincts are by reconnecting with your body. The loss of connection has led many people to an early grave. Any behaviour that no longer serves you is detrimental to your health.

Is your mind healthy? Is your body healthy? The goal is to figure out how to answer yes to both of these questions. If you answer no to even one of those questions, then that's a sure sign that making small changes will positively benefit you even if it comes at the cost of throwing some tasty eggs and bacon directly into the bin.

INTERVIEW HIGHLIGHTS FROM SPEAKER, AUTHOR, AND COACH, TONY GASKINS

Somewhere around 2015 I was scrolling around Twitter and happened upon a photo meme of a quote that read: *If you don't build the life of your dreams someone will hire you to build theirs for them.* I remember being so moved by these words I proceeded to screenshot the meme and filed it in my phone under the folder motivational quotes.

A few years passed and I was researching potential podcast guests and I came across the name, Tony Gaskins. Tony Gaskins is a public speaker, author, and life coach. He's appeared on The Oprah Winfrey Show, The Tyra Banks Show and TBN's 700 Club. He speaks on various topics including business, success and self-development but is most known for his love and relationship advice for men which has garnered him a large Facebook, Instagram, and Twitter following. In 2011, he made Under30CEO's *Top 50 Most Motivational People on the Web.*

Having done my due diligence, I discovered he was the guy who penned the quote I had saved years prior. I found his contact and scheduled an interview which turned out to be very enlightening for me on multiple levels. Tony is a guy who comes from humble beginnings and through hard work and determination have built quite the life for himself and his family. I mean, he was on Oprah! What else is there to say?

The following conversation between myself and Tony Gaskins took place on September 19th, 2018, while Tony was a guest on my podcast *Ungoogleable*:

My Question: [referencing tapping into his intuition in relation to figuring out his bigger purpose] When did you understand that you were capable of helping so many people and from there, how did you know which route to take?

Tony's Answer: You know, I kind of had a blind faith. I guess I was ignorant to an extent. The funny thing is that it benefited me because I didn't know how hard it is to impact millions of people. I literally just started doing it. I trusted myself and my gut feelings. I didn't know how it would happen or when it would happen, but kind of putting one foot in front of the other, seeing what options were available to me.

I found Facebook, I found Myspace, I found Twitter and just started learning the different outlets and how to use my voice in those spaces and just doing it consistently every day. It just started to grow and grow and grow and it grew organically. It knocked my socks off. My intuition has never led me astray, somehow, it already knows the answers that I'm seeking.

My Question: [referencing how to apply the lessons we learn about ourselves in order to give back] How would you teach the knowledge that you've gained about yourself and about the world to a room full of fourteen-year-olds?

Tony's Answer: One of my friends said, 'Tony, I have holes in my socks.' I was like, 'What do you mean?' and he said, 'You can't see my problems.'

I feel part of the issue with society is that it's hard for us to teach the youth, if the adults teaching the classes have 'holes in their socks.' Because we don't really know, it's hard for us to teach the fourteen-year-olds but what I would say to the fourteen-year-old boys is that, inside of every man there's a lion and a lamb.

One lesson I learned when I was a toxic and controlling boyfriend, was from my sister.

Her boyfriend was a thug—and he was a *real* street thug, he was a thief, and a scary dude. My sister told me once, she said, 'Tony, with everything bad that he does, and he fights all the time with other men, I've never seen him lose a street fight, but he's never put one hand on me. He's never yelled at me, and he's never cursed at me.'

And at that point, when I found out that this hardened criminal, this thug was gentle with her, that every night when they went to bed they would hold each other, I learned the lesson of balance between the lion and the lamb. My point is: You have to know when to be strong, when to be tough and more importantly, when to trust yourself.

INTERVIEW HIGHLIGHTS FROM SPORTS SCIENTIST AND PROFESSOR, DR COREY PEACOCK

I have to be honest with you, I started interviewing successful teachers, athletes and entrepreneurs to initially attempt to figure out what I was doing wrong in my life. I thought to myself, *If I can ask the proper questions then maybe I can figure out how I can further succeed and progress.*

At the time, I didn't realise the importance of creating new relationships and how that is equally as important to our wellbeing as is knowledge is to progress. Having done over five hundred interviews sometimes guests become friends and, in this case, I consider Corey a mate.

I first interviewed Corey in 2016 when he was working with the famed MMA gym in South Florida called The Blackzilians. Fast forward seven years, and few rebrands, and Corey is now the head sports science guy with Kill Cliff MMA as well as a professor. Dr Corey Peacock is the Head Performance Coach and Sports Scientist at Peacock Performance Inc. Corey graduated from Kent State University with a Ph.D. in Exercise Physiology. He works closely with many professional athletes from the NFL, NHL, MMA and NCAAF and is regarded as one of the top Performance Coaches and Sports Scientists in the United States. Along with coaching, Dr Peacock also serves as an Associate Professor in the Department of Health and Human Performance at Nova Southeastern University, Florida.

Having been an athlete himself and also being from Northeast Ohio, I trust his word in regard to human performance. With us living in a noisy social media world where everyone seems to be an expert, Corey is one of the few brilliant minds I lean on when I need proper answers and information about the complexity of movement relating to the human body.

The following conversation between myself and Dr Corey Peacock took place on November 12th, 2018, while Corey was a guest on my podcast *Ungoogleable:*

My Question: [referencing the role skill and talent plays in relation to performance outcomes with championship calibre fighters/athletes] I recently heard a famous coach speak publicly about not having their fighters powerlift or weight train eight weeks out from their fight. I wanted to know then, how much of an athlete's success is genetics and how much is coaching? With endless dogma from coaches and pro athletes already performing on such high levels, is superior athletic performance the result of the athlete or a result of the evolution of sports science?

Corey's Answer: I'll truly say, and I really believe this, a champion is a champion for a reason. There is only so much you can do with somebody at that calibre to help them improve.

You know, me as a sports scientist and strength and conditioning coach, I can have somebody, for instance, I have Michael Chandler who just started camp and he's fighting for the Bellator lightweight world title. Listen, if I can implement the smallest amount of strength and conditioning into his program to help promote, you know… recovery, to help prevent injuries, to help maintain if not, just slightly increase, power and strength then I've done my job with somebody like that.

Because with or without me, he is a world champion in every aspect of his life, that's just something he has worked his ass off for years to get to that level.

My Question: What about things that we can't measure? Like intuition, I know you're a science guy, but we can't measure instincts or a fighter's intuitive ability to avoid damage, you can't measure someone's "heart" or their will to overcome, their "fighter spirit". What's your stance on these [sort] of immeasurable components?

Corey's Answer: You know, Jonny, sports science can get overwhelming. I have a data analyst who helps me with all the data that I've collected over the years. Talking about that "heart", how does somebody do those things that they're capable of doing?

I'll be honest, a V02 Max test will show you a lot of things that are different with fighters in comparison to other professional athletes. There are points in the physiological state when you're looking at the assessment where the body is telling you or that the test is telling you that human body should shut down and that they can't continue to go on, but yet these fighters have the ability to hit an unknown gear and maintain it for another ninety seconds to two minutes.

Somebody like Michael Chandler, Michael can hit numbers on these tests where most normal people will pass out and die like climbing Mt Everest and he can hit that point and sustain that at an even higher degree for at least another two to three minutes. That's one of those things, again it's measurable, but you ask yourself, Where is that coming from? I mean, is it really just his physiological state? Or is there something different with his mind or instincts that we as scientists still don't know how to measure that allows him to do that.

I do believe in that. I believe there are things in these special athletes that are not measurable, there are instincts, there's heart, there's things up there in that complex structure known as the brain that we don't have the ability to measure properly.

HABIT THREE: ACTION PLAN

Pay attention to your daily caloric intake if you dare to lose weight. Awareness is crucial. I started doing this roughly five years ago. The point of saying "F$&k breakfast" isn't about me telling you that I know a magic way to lose weight, there is no magic way. What I'm telling you is to challenge yourself to rethink how you view your daily meals, especially if you're overweight.

My current window frame of eating starts at one pm and finishes at seven pm. That's an eighteen hour window of not eating or six total hours to consume the highest grade of nutrient dense foods that I can find. I suggest you start with a fourteen-hour window of not eating. It's important to keep this structure consistent both with your sleep patterns (which I'll get into later) as well as your wake up times. This will properly give your digestive systems a routine which will allow you to maintain constant high energy levels throughout the day. Consistency is key. Start with fourteen hours of not eating and eight hours of consuming.

For example, let's say you go to bed at ten pm and wake up at six am. Your first caloric intake should be at twelve pm, this gives you ten whole hours to consume the healthiest foods possible. What works for me to balance cravings and hunger are the consumption of water and staying active. Your body wants to move and to sweat, but it won't take long for your systems to adjust to these minor changes.

Be disciplined in your approach and write things down! Document when you go to bed, write down when you wake up, and from there create a plan of attack for when your next meals will be. Give it a week, you'll get used to it by then.

In the next chapter you'll learn more skills and tips on how to manage your food intake throughout the day both from a physical standpoint and more importantly, from a psychological perspective. Food is fuel, not entertainment. I only eat foods that make me feel good, nothing that slows me down.

Reminder: if you have to read it, don't eat it. What does that even mean? Simply put, the more steps it takes for your food to reach your plate, the less healthy it is. Think about a piece of salmon from the seafood market that you pair with a sweet potato or asparagus. Not a ton of steps, right? Now think about any of your favourite microwavable meals such as mac 'n' cheese or a frozen pizza. Read the ingredients on the back. Can you pronounce those words? How many steps did that meal take to reach your plate versus the salmon? Finally, what do you call that meal? Is it dinner? Lunch? Breakfast? Is it supposed to have a name? Maybe? Maybe not?

CHAPTER FOUR

HABIT FOUR: REFRAME YOU MEALS

WHAT DOES IT MEAN TO REFRAME?

Reframe: ADJECTIVE: The ability to express words or concepts differently.

'You are what you are and where you are because of what has gone into your mind. You can change what you are and where you are by changing what goes into your mind.[11]'
— Zig Ziglar

From the minute I first read this quote I loved it. I wasn't coaching at the time, but I was inquisitive. It was in my last semester of a leadership grad program in Las Vegas, Nevada when I learned about Zig Ziglar, and his words deeply resonated with me.

The course I was taking was all about breaking down mental barriers we had constructed in our lives since childhood, with the purpose of progressing through them. I wasn't the architect of these walls and boundaries. Most of these barriers were given to me when I was a child by adults who knew no better.

They're everywhere, these limiting belief systems that imprison us. They can be in the form of social constructs such as gender-

---
11 Ziglar, n.d., para. 4

based activities, for example: you're a little boy so you should be playing with cars and toy trains, things like that. You get my point. These constructs manifest in other ways, from the clothes we wear and even with the foods we eat. These barriers, if allowed, become responsible for static life experiences and excuse filled realities.

Great writers and thinkers have an exceptional gift of enabling their audiences to adopt their words and/or philosophies to match one's individual experiences. Revisiting this quote allows me to reframe Zig's words and place them into my own personal story. As a health and wellness coach, I always switch out the words 'are' for 'eat', 'where' for 'who', and 'mind' with 'body'. Now it reads: 'You are what you eat and who you are because of what has gone into your body.' See now, it's my quote (refer to the reframe definition above if I've lost you).

I'd like to think Zig would be proud of how I've reframed his words. If you're unfamiliar with Ziglar, here's a quick summary of the wiseman's resume: Zig Ziglar is one of the most successful motivational speakers of all time. He came from an era of despair, born into the late 1920s and was raised in the southern part of the United States during the Great Depression. He tapped into something deeply personal within himself and had the gumption to take his passion and help the world. It's fair to say my grandpa's motivational speakers were built a bit differently than the ones today. You know the type today: big talk, broody looking, loud, and standing on stage while they tell you how much your life sucks. As if you didn't know that already? Before you know it, you're giving away thousands of dollars to be part of a secret mastermind group. Alright, now you understand a little more about Zig, let's refocus the chat back to you! To recap: you've woken up, you didn't press snooze, you made your bed, and you're on a winning streak, you're creating positive momentum for the day. You leave your bedroom, and you go into the kitchen. You drink a tall glass of water; you turn the coffee machine on and let it get warmed up. You go into the bathroom, floss your teeth, then you make your coffee. While you allow it to cool off a little bit, you put your clothes on, put your deodorant on, wash your face, wash your hands. Drink the coffee, now you brush your teeth. You're all set; ready to rock and roll, and take on your day.

By now, you've realised what this is. You're learning about the benefits daily systems provide and the simplicity there is in a healthy morning routine. These processes are sustainable daily habits that you will be able to carry with you now up until you get old and grey. Fad diets, fitness rends, starving yourself from calories, all those things may work for a small amount of time, but they are gimmicks; they're not sustainable.

These systems I'm sharing with you are easy, applicable and practical habits you will carry with you throughout the rest of your life and guess what? We haven't spent a dime on any of them. Well… maybe the coffee. I'm fancy and quality coffee beans are a bit of a vice of mine. Alright, so the day is starting to progress, let's fast forward; we will say it's eleven am. You still haven't eaten yet. I mentioned this earlier, this is what I call our "Digestive Reset".

DISCLAIMER: I'm not a doctor. Before you begin any new physical training or accept any nutritional advice, please make sure that your doctor gives you the go ahead.

My one-on-one private coaching clientele base in Sydney, Australia is made up of people who come to me to lose weight, get strong, and get healthy. Most of these people have never been at their optimal health before. Why do you think that is? The answer is simple, two words: Eating Habits.

My eight years of coaching has taught me one valuable lesson: Losing weight is hard, but what's even harder is teaching people new habits and a new perspective on what and how they should be eating. Remember when we were talking about social constructs in relation to mental barriers? This the tie into this area of the book.

Many of us, myself included, have been taught erroneous, toxic eating habits. We don't need to eat everything on our plates. We don't need to eat until we are full. What we need is to teach ourselves how to reframe our meals, how we mentally understand the words we use to correlate and attach to our meals (I'll explain more about that in a second).

If your body weight is something you have always struggled with, if you have never been to your goal weight on the scales, if you have never felt energised, if you do not know what it's like to feel amazing, then you must make a change. Do it now. We live in a culture where so many of us get so comfortable with living uncomfortable and that breaks my heart. I want everybody I care for, everybody I know, and now all you guys reading this, to understand what it's like to feel amazing.

We must reframe what we were taught as kids in relationship to our food. My point is we do not have to label our meals. We have already done away with breakfast, breakfast the word, break it down, break your fast, we are going to say *fuck that*. I am going to continue my fast throughout the day. I should clarify, I am not antifood. I am not a maniac, food is our fuel, but that is exactly what it is. Somewhere along the lines, we have confused food with entertainment, but food is our subsistence and is the key to our life. It is the engine that drives us, it is the fuel that sparks our activity.

Lunch? No. Lunch is the time you eat food. Dinner? No. Dinner is a time you eat food. Throw these words out of your vocabulary now, you do not need to use the word lunch, you do not need to use the word dinner. Reframe your meals, choose a time and a window of when you eat and then eat at that time.

As I mentioned in the last chapter, here's what works for me: I eat from one pm to seven pm. After that a six-hour window, I give my body eighteen hours to reset (that 'digestive reset' I spoke about earlier). The next day there's another six hours to eat what I want. Some days are better than others, but over time what you are going to do is teach yourself the value of eating high quality nutrient dense foods. That is, foods high in quality macronutrients; proteins including chicken, beef, fish, pork; good carbohydrates like sweet potatoes and rice; good fats, avocados and whichever nuts you prefer (my favourite is cashews).

Here's the rule of thumb, ask yourself the next time you eat: How many steps did this food take to get to my plate? It doesn't have to be confusing, and it doesn't have to be tricky or even scientific. The fewer the steps the better. Also, if you must read the label on your food, don't eat it. If you must read it, don't eat it. Why? Because it's processed.

Back to my timeframe of eating, it doesn't have to be one pm to seven pm, that's just what I do now and I am probably going to stick with that as long as I can. When I started on this journey, I started at ten am to seven pm, so my window was nine hours.

That worked for a while but then I realised I didn't really need to be eating at ten am and so kept pushing it back and over the last two years I've discovered one pm is perfect for me.

Later in the book, I will go over in detail my full day but for now let's grasp the practicality of reframing our meals. On paper it's simple. You don't need to romanticise your food by labelling your meals throughout your day. When we put names on things, we label them, we marginalise them, we put ourselves in a box, we limit our potential, we stop thinking for ourselves and more importantly we lose the sense of acknowledgment of the things we're doing to our own bodies. We only get one. Let's all be a little more aware of how we treat it. At the end of the day, our bodies are a direct result of our habits. You have the power to change both. Believe in that, because I do.

It's perfectly healthy to experience many different changes of perspective throughout one's life. You should be worried if you don't. Settling for what always has been, just because it's always been that way is a common form of tapping out in life. Options are all around you. If you need to make a change, then do it. Experiment with things, challenge your normalcy and be determined while doing it.

One of my favourite personal mantras that I say when I wake up is: You can do a lot of things that you can't do. Sit with those words for a second and tell me if I'm wrong with what I'm about to say, but who's holding you back right now? The things that you keep putting off, who told you in the first place that you can't do them? I'm guessing no one told you; you told yourself you couldn't and now it's time to tell yourself that you can.

INTERVIEW HIGHLIGHTS FROM
ULTRA-ENDURANCE ATHLETE, RICH ROLL

I mentioned earlier in the book that I've always been intrigued by those who do things that I choose not to do. I'm fascinated with human potential. I love watching big wave surfing, but you won't catch me dead in open water deeper than my waist. I'm a fan of free solo mountain climbing but I've never hung from the edge of a cliff. Sports like motorcycle racing and bull riding are most impressive to me, but I've never driven a motorcycle at high speeds or dared attempt to ride a bull. You understand my point, rather than shying away from my insecurities I'm fascinated by them.

This inquisition led me to a former successful California attorney turned Vegan Ultra Marathon runner named Rich Roll. A graduate of Stanford University and Cornell Law School, Rich is an accomplished vegan ultra-endurance athlete and former entertainment attorney turned full-time wellness and plant-based nutrition advocate, popular public speaker, husband, father of four and inspiration to people worldwide as a transformative example of courageous and healthy living. In 2012, Rich became a #1 bestselling author with the publication of his inspirational memoir: *Finding Ultra: Rejecting Middle Age, Becoming One of the World's Fittest Men and Discovering Myself.* Picking up where the book leaves off, in 2013 Rich launched the wildly popular *Rich Roll Podcast*, which consistently sits atop the iTunes top ten list.

In his forties he shifted gears in his life to attain a more healthy and positive future. I reached out to him with the sole intention of learning from a man who was known for reframing his mindset.

The following conversation between myself and Rich Roll took place on May 15th, 2018 while Rich was a guest on my podcast *Ungoogleable:*

My Question: [In regard to his success and mental framework] Of all the labels and titles that you have created for yourself: athlete, speaker, wellness advocate, can you share with me what you feel your most notable strengths are regarding your continuous success in multiple industries?

Rich's Answer: I don't think [it's] talent. I think my strengths are my ability to withstand discomfort. This has served me well as an endurance athlete but also has probably led me into some bad directions in my life. I have a high pain threshold and I focus and work hard; I was never the smartest guy or the best student or the most talented athlete, but I figured out early on how to outwork everybody and make my way that way and that served me well as well in terms of what I've done athletically. The books I've written have used that blueprint so I've been able to have the podcast too, although it does bring up balance issues for me that I continue to struggle to master.

My Question: Doing these ultra-endurance events, these one hundred plus mile events that are out of the normalcy realm of the average person, who would you say these types of events targets? What type of person and what type of mindset?

Rich's Answer: Well, I think you must be a little bit off your rocker. You must be a different sort of thinker, you know, how you frame things around you and what you feel your reality needs to consist of. It's excruciatingly painful and it requires a tremendous amount of time that sort of monopolises your life. I think that the people that gravitates towards it or are magnetised by this world, in my experience, tend to be people who… first, there's no money in it, there's no fame or glory, really most of these races take place without anybody paying attention and without any media attention whatsoever. You got to do it because you love it and the people that love it are really looking for something more than just a physical challenge. What they're really looking for is a better self-understanding and that's what got me into it.

I was struggling with my career and my place in the world, and I was looking for an opportunity to not only test my physical limits but to really explore the parameters of my mental and emotional and spiritual being. When you're doing ultra-endurance sports it strips you down to the core. The closest thing that I can imagine it's like is an ayahuasca trip, you really meet your maker, and it forces you to grapple with who you are. It's a template for personal growth.

For me, it was never about how fast I was or how many people I can beat, or can I win this race and stand on a podium. I wanted to understand myself and it seemed like a big template for exploring that, so you see a lot of people in this world who is kind of doing the same thing.

INTERVIEW HIGHLIGHTS FROM ENTREPRENEUR, TOM BILYEU

When I first started coaching, I worked at a health club in Sydney with a real estate business model. For the owners, the gym was a bank system disguised as a health club. For me and the other thirty personal trainers, we paid rent to work there and were given access to the health club's attendees with hopes of turning human connections into paid clients. This was the most toxic work environment I've ever experienced. Who would think working at a health club would be detrimental to one's mental stability but trust me when I say, when thirty coaches are put into a room with their livelihood on the line in terms of living expenses, rent, and security you'll see the worst side of people. This was my first experience working in the fitness industry.

I gained a bunch of weight due to an addiction to protein bars and shakes. This led me to research other alternatives for eating healthy snacks and I stumbled upon a brand called Quest Bars. I was instantly hooked since they didn't cause any bloating in my gut and something about the ingredients were satiating. I wasn't left hungry an hour later like all the other bars I had tried. My natural mind wanted to chat with the owner and ask a few questions so I did some digging, used my podcast as a ploy and set up a chat with the CEO Tom.

Tom Bilyeu is the co-founder of 2014 Inc. 500 company Quest Nutrition—a unicorn startup valued at over $1 billion—and the co-founder and host of the popular interview based show *Impact Theory*. Tom's mission is the creation of empowering media-based IP and the acceleration of mission-based businesses. Personally, driven to help people develop the skills they will need to improve themselves and the world, Tom is determined to use commerce to address the dual pandemics of physical and mental malnourishment.

The following conversation between myself and Tom Bilyeu took place on February 21st, 2018, while Tom was a guest on my podcast *Ungoogleable*:

My Question: When you guys were initially getting the rolling with Quest Nutrition what was the heartbeat? What was the drive behind starting it and can you talk a little bit about how that initial motivation has changed as your company has grown?

Tom's Answer: In the early days, it really was in many ways a reaction to the company that we had before this which was a technology company called, 'Awareness Tech' and we were making money, winning awards, and standing at one point in this beautiful conference room looking at the Pacific Ocean and we turned to each other and said, 'Man, there has to be a better way to do business.' [We wanted] something that's focused on value creation, something that we really believe in that we have a lot of passion about and while we founded the company for three very different reasons, if we were to look at a diagram, the area that really overlaps in our personal passions was nutrition, so that became the path that we were going down.

My business partner Ron is just as insanely talented at nutrition, what he knows about human metabolism is ridiculous so it was just an exciting chance to leverage a lot of his talents and skills. For me, growing up in a morbidly obese family, it was an opportunity to really help them and when you really look at the problem it's a pandemic at this point.

When you look at what the solution is, telling people to eat less and to exercise more works for a narrow band of people and for people who are willing to do that then they get in amazing shape, they look incredible, they're healthy as the day is long, but for the vast majority of people, food is really something that they eat for pleasure way more than sustenance and so I felt like we really understood something that the food industry really didn't get which is, if you really want to get people to comply with something that's healthy then you must give them food that they can choose based on taste and the healthy part must come along for the ride. So, that was what we focused on.

We made snacks and other food items that people could eat because they wanted to and that they were really excited about, and we were doing the hard work to make sure that it was healthy for you.

HABIT FOUR: ACTION PLAN

Now look, if losing weight has always been a difficult task for you then I suggest you take your time with this habit and slowly make small and minor adjustments. Your relationship with food is a personal one and if you're overweight then it's also a psychological one.

People overeat for various reasons; some people are confused about portion size, some eat as an emotional trigger, some are simply uneducated about nutrition. If any of these reasons resonate with you, don't feel bad about it. Your general practitioner or family doctor probably doesn't have a degree in nutrition. It's not even a mandatory field of study for students to learn if they want to become doctors, point being, many people are lost and confused when it comes to the food on their plate and overall knowledge of what to eat and what not to eat. Creating a plan and structure will be key for you to make changes in this department.

What works for me is writing things down. I create strategies around my food from the time I wake up in the morning all the way until I fall asleep. Because I'm habitual overeater I also only shop for the meals that I'm preparing that day, I'll never "stock my fridge" this allows me to never overindulge, it also allows me to maintain a healthy relationship with food. I don't expect you to do this step-by-step, most of you have kids, a family and loved ones. It's not conducive for you to only shop for the meals that you're preparing that day but what is conducive is for you to experiment with a routine different from what you're doing now. Whatever you adjust to, do it on the weekends as well, don't allow your discipline during the week to be sabotaged.

I suggest you start with your work week, Monday through Friday, and go from there. Remove the words "breakfast", "lunch" and "dinner" from your nutritional vernacular and replace them with "times when I choose to eat" this way you won't feel obligated to stuff your face during those moments when lunchtime comes around and you're not even hungry, you eat because you've always been conditioned to do so, not anymore, you're done with that, now you choose to eat when you feel like it.

Create your meals with the most nutrient dense foods possible. Food is fuel, not entertainment, it either makes us feel like shit or makes us feel energised, the decision and outcome is totally up to you and the choices that you make.

Earlier I mentioned the word "awareness". This is a key word to fully comprehend moving forward when thinking about your overall health. Be aware of the beverages that you choose to drink, be aware of the calories that you choose to consume. Catch yourself during moments of mindless eating; snacking is for children.

Adults don't snack, they mindlessly eat. Be aware of this, it's f#%king hard to live a healthy lifestyle, anyone who says it isn't probably is trying to sell you something. You're fooling yourself by thinking that being healthy is a gift, it's f#%king not, you must earn a healthy lifestyle. Hopefully it doesn't take a health scare for you to understand this. Feeling great about yourself and being a role model to the people around you should be your number one goal. Shouldn't it? Nothing worth talking about is ever gifted to us, is it? Aren't the most important things in life earned through discipline and practice? Earned. Not given. Wouldn't you agree that to feel accomplished about anything effort is required? I'm hoping you say yes…

CHAPTER FIVE

HABIT FIVE: EARN YOUR KEEP

WHAT IS EFFORT?

Effort: NOUN: A vigorous or determined attempt at something. A force exerted by oneself or within a process.

'Satisfaction lies within the effort not in the attainment. Full effort is full victory.'
— Mahatma Gandhi[12]

Before we get this chapter going, I must clarify that I didn't use a Gandhi quote as an attempt to proclaim myself as a humanitarian or as an enlightened man. I was hesitant to use this quote due to the obvious projection the name Gandhi makes. To be honest, if I wanted to be a douche bag, I would have used the standard Instagram famous quote of Gandhi's that every "Fitness Influencer" uses – 'Be the change that you want to see in the world'… Vomit. The quote is brilliant, it's the half-naked model posing in promiscuous stances that bother me.

Where do people get off using such powerful and important words so recklessly as bait to pull people into their realities?

---

12   Gandhi, 1957, p. 36.

You know, the shaved body type with tanning oil doused all over their skin posing in sexual gratifying positions; do these people not know there's a thing called the internet? Am I supposed to believe this naked person in this photo with one million followers constructed these words? Well shit, with the state of the modern landscape regarding the average persons' health and wellness… maybe.

Who are we supposed to believe? Who are we supposed to follow? And better yet, who are we supposed to take advice from? All three questions are extremely important and with improper guidance and direction, you could end up in a situation with your friends regurgitating a Gandhi quote and telling you that 'Jimmy Instagram' said it. I can't let this happen; I got your back.

Let's all make a deal from now on moving forward; we will all work our asses off physically, mentally and spiritually to better put ourselves in positions of trust. Trust, you ask? Yes, trust in yourself. The more you take your health and wellness seriously the more you will tap into your instincts and the less you will search outside of yourself. This is a natural progression with those who get healthy. They start learning the languages of their bodies, they start understanding what real energy is and what real strength is. A beautiful thing starts to happen; the absence of second guessing yourself. This will show up in many other areas of your life, not just during your workouts.

Now to my point: our lives are reflections of our efforts. We become what we do, and we feel how we think. Gandhi's words are a manifest of his personal experiences. This man knew what it was like to struggle and sacrifice. He knew what unbridled effort meant and he showed his heart off to the world. You'd be hard pressed to find another example of optimal leadership than Gandhi.

As an Indian immigrant in the early 1900s in South Africa, he famously protested freedom. He then went on to be the face of India during its Independence movement from Great Britain. His message was minimalistic and peaceful. He was known to possess nothing yet so many people followed him. He became immortalised for his hunger strikes and protests. His mission in India was to bring peace to all people, but specifically to the Hindus and Muslims. Even after being assassinated, ground accounting to over one million people flocked to his burial. Why? What made him such a great leader? His message was always about unity and peace. He felt wars could be won without firing a single bullet. Ideas like his were deemed radical but people still listened. It was through his actions that made his people believe and trust in him. The congruence he had between his actions and messaging was undeniable.

This is the crux of it, great leaders lead with their ears not their words, and it's the lessons learned through listening to the words that enable the leader to act accordingly. He never shouted for people to follow him; he simply walked on silently and the people came.

I feel I needed to use such an intense example of effort to highlight the relevance it has on our life. This works both ways as well, it's the age-old story of two men; one man with devout effort and little to no means can change the world while the other man with endless opportunities waste away choosing a life of inadequacy. A stark contrast with dramatic outcomes. How have you earned your keep today? Have you tested yourself physically or mentally or are you just getting by on the two legs and two arms that were given to you by your parents? We didn't earn this body; it was a gift. How do you take care of gifts that are offered to you? How do you take care of your body? It's an interesting concept, the fact so many of us take our bodies and our health for granted. We eat what we want, we move when we want, we think how we want, what a beautiful and wonderful concept. An important question is: why are so many of us upset with life? Why are so many people obese and unfulfilled? Are we not appreciative of this opportunity that was gifted to us?

I recently had a client tell me when I challenged him on his weight that he was *trying*. I fucking hate that word. Sorry for the language but nothing is more base level minded than the person who uses the word *try*. You either do or you don't mate, there is no such thing as "try" – even Yoda knew that. I asked him, how much weight did he lose this week? He turned to me and went, 'I didn't lose anything.' I then go, 'Well, where else do you think we can make some changes? This is two weeks in a row where your weight has stayed the same.'

I must tell you guys something before we continue, this guy needs to lose probably twenty more kilos. He has already lost five kilos but another twenty is a must! He's in his fifties, his life is on the line, people rely on him. He runs multiple companies; he has a family. Due to his bodyweight, he's putting his life expectancy at risk.

He then turns to me, and he goes, 'Well I do not know Jonny, I work out with you five times a week, I don't know why I'm not losing the weight!' I turned to him, and I go, 'How dare you. Working out is only the first step, you cannot get to where you want to go just by working out!'

You can't expect to get healthy if you have always been overweight simply by working out. If you're obese and weight loss is a goal of yours, just working out isn't enough, it's a key and crucial step I call, "sweat equity". Just as you would put equity into a business or an idea, you need to put equity into your body and your physical wellbeing, and the currency is sweat!

This is probably the most uncomfortable part of the book for most of you. Right now, I want you to stop reading and stand up and go look at yourself in the mirror. Are you happy with what you see? If not, what are you going to do about it to change?

Psychologists call this process "self-reflection" therapy. They ask their clients to stand in front of a mirror and have a conversation with themselves. The patient talks about things that bother them, issues in their life that have become quite intense, and areas of their behaviour. They feel a change is a must and then they prioritise these reflections. They write them down and they talk about them frequently. They don't push them to the side and pretend that they don't exist. Sound familiar?

How many people that you love are overweight? Have you asked them about it? Are you overweight? Do your loved ones ask you about it? As a culture, we need to change the narrative around unhealthy lifestyles and start creating the conversation towards the people that we love. Think about it, if your brother is an addict or alcoholic, I guarantee you and your family at some point will intervene and offer your support and encouragement. Why doesn't this happen with our loved ones who are overweight and obese? Why do we brush it under the rug? Are we not aware these people are dying?

The person who's addicted to substances is no different than the person who's addicted to food. The brain chemistry is the same, the cravings are the same, the only difference is the variable. One turns to the drug while the other turns to food. Each one finds comfort in their chosen vice while their loved ones are forced to sit-back and watch. It goes back to my earlier point about so many of us live lives being comfortable with feeling uncomfortable about ourselves.

Getting deep, aren't we? Let's go back to the self-reflection mirror work, I do this process quite often at my house. Here's how you can do it. I talk to myself about my goals, I talk to myself about current projects, and I talk to myself about things that either make me happy or sad. In this case, I want you to use this technique to self-motivate yourself. You have everything you need to get healthy already within yourself, you just need to commit and take action.

Clients often come to me with questions surrounding their goals and want my advice on how they can achieve them. I use an easy technique I've come up with called the IVC principle. We must first *Identify* the goal we are seeking, then we must *Visualise* ourselves achieving that goal and finally we must *Commit* to a strategy or plan of attack that will enable us in reaching that goal. Look, I'm aware of the difficulties of making changes as well as the fear placed on moving the body in relation to getting healthy.

Being vulnerable is a tough task and joining a gym can be extremely daunting. I hate gyms, it's the crowds that bother me. I don't like egos, loud music or anxiety driven people with their head on a swivel trying to catch a glance at every piece of action walking by. I still go. I like feeling good about myself knowing that I chose to do something that I didn't enjoy. I hate the process of training but I love the outcomes. I hate lacing my running shoes up, but I love the sweat that's produced after a fifteen kilometre run. I hate fighting but I love the sense of accomplishment after sparring with another man for twelve rounds in a boxing ring. It's life's cruel secret, it's the only path to true happiness, a law of nature, for there to be resistance before retribution.

DISCLAIMER: I am not a doctor, so before you engage in any fitness routines consult your general practitioner just so they could give you the go ahead that you are fit enough to take part in a physical fitness routine.

Your effort equals your outcomes. Stop expecting to see changes for the better if you haven't put forth the time and energy. The worst trick you can play on yourself is telling yourself that "they got lucky" or "they only have that because someone gave it to them". Guess what? There is no luck. You only see the end results of the people you cheer for; you never see the path and the effort. Anyone that you either despise due to fame or cheer for due to your loyalty has put in the effort. Nothing great comes from stagnant minds and bodies. There can't be any real progress without honest effort.

INTERVIEW HIGHLIGHTS FROM BODYBUILDING LEGEND, JAY CUTLER

Insights on Jay Cutler: It's no secret that I'm an 80s baby. That territory comes with a lot of culture. Born in the early 80s and a teen by the mid-90s, I was exposed to many different iconic cultural shifts. Madonna taught me that sex wasn't the devil as Prince showed me that every man, if given the proper wardrobe, has the potential of owning a stage. Boxing delivered Ray "Boom Boom" Mancini to my dining room as I sketched within the lines of his fight poses printed in my colouring books as Pay Per View TV allowed me to watch legal and public executions via Mike Tyson or what they sold them to us as alleged boxing matches. Music, movies, art and sports seemed to be everywhere but nothing was as big as The Terminator. This guy was fictitious superhero but he was real.

Those seeds were planted and as I manoeuvred through adulthood, I always seemed to keep my eye on the real life superheroes, I'm talking about bodybuilders. Many of these guys come and go like the icons I mentioned earlier, but one of them just seemed to never go away. The sport of bodybuilding is fickle, only one person ever wins the highest award, titled Mr Olympia, yet the tragedy lies within the athletes who finish second or third. A close non-first place finish usually means the end of one's career, but word kept spreading about this one guy who was repeatedly finishing second and not retiring. Then one day after many years of losing and coming back for more he won. People were shocked and elated for him. This is Jay Cutler. Imagine the mindset he developed through the years of disappointment. Jay Cutler is a retired American professional bodybuilder. A IFBB pro, he is a four-time Mr Olympia winner, having won in 2006, 2007, 2009, and 2010.

The following conversation between myself and Jay Cutler took place on April 25th, 2018, while Jay was a guest on my podcast *Ungoogleable:*

My Question: I think it was about ten years ago now when I saw a YouTube video of yours and you were in your house, and you were hustling with your t-shirt line. You were in your house in Vegas, you were in the middle of your pro career getting ready for the Mr Olympia contest and you were doing the clothing line out of the house, you were selling supps out of the house, and then to watch you evolve as an athlete and entrepreneur; what's it like looking back on all your efforts in relation to the success that you've created for yourself?

Jay's Answer: I can recall before the internet I started doing mail orders. I had one shirt, one eight by ten picture. I wasn't even a pro yet, and people would write to me with a PO Box from all the magazines. You must remember, that was our only outlet at the time, so if people wanted me to respond and communicate with them, they would handwrite me letters. These weren't typed letters, these weren't emails, the internet didn't exist yet, so they would send me letters and I'd say okay, I'd write them hand letters back and I would put in there just a photocopy sheet. I had the picture on there, the t-shirt on there and I'd write and say if you want to purchase this send me a check or money order. They would send me cash.

That's how I financed myself in the beginning of my career, I thought to myself, 'Wow, I think there's something here', then of course I started doing DVDs then I did books, then I did t-shirts. I remember starting the t-shirt line in 2008, that's when I really started to take off. Then I started the Cutler Athletics Brand, the Swole Monkey brand and was selling t-shirts out of my garage and I did that all the way until a year ago.

Then I got a warehouse space in Vegas. Shoot, I was selling half a million bucks a year out of my garage, this was before social media. I remember doing DVDs, I tell people I had probably ten people, close friends and girlfriends, guys that I knew that were helping me pack up the DVDs. I launched a DVD once a year, I filmed one every year for each preparation, I had five different releases I did, and I remember those things would sell, I would sell thousands in the first week. It was a lot; people were looking forward to them. I would do ads in the magazines, this is when print ads mattered, people would watch the DVD release and the orders would start flying in overnight and overseas was crazy, they would order up the DVDs, I was selling them for forty bucks each, I'm grateful for the fans and for the outcomes of those years of effort.

One last thing about Jay. I must shout out my beautiful and talented girlfriend, Christina, who was with me the night I interviewed Jay. I asked her to serve as my cameraman due to Jay being in town for the Sydney Fit Expo. If you must know, I can be a shy person if the circumstances aren't in my favour.

The short version, Jay and I had been back and forth for weeks via Instagram messaging setting up a time and place for our podcast. I knew the hotel he was staying at and we also booked a specific night but as the event drew near, he went silent on me. No confirmation of the interview, no text reply, nothing. The organiser in me, maybe it's more neurotic than anything, either way, puts me in a position to send a confirmation email the night leading up to each interview even if it's already booked in. It's a system I've always used since I started podcasting. I like being prepared and that confirmation from the guest is my last point of reference before I film, it puts me at ease to say the least.

Okay, so Chrissie and I show up at the hotel and we see Jay in the hall with a group of fans signing autographs I then look at Chrissie and say, 'You know what Chris, he didn't respond to my confirmation message, let's just get out of here.'

She then turns to me and says, 'You must be crazy! I didn't come all the way down here carrying your equipment for you to just go home, you better go approach him now and let him know you're here.' I obviously needed her support and advice at this moment because that little push led us towards accomplishing the goal of the interview. I had a blast getting to know Jay and learning from him, but old habits die hard. As a boy I had a huge inferiority complex and in that moment with Jay, I almost allowed it to creep back into my life and consume me. Never undervalue the importance of accountability with strong and healthy relationships.

INTERVIEW HIGHLIGHTS FROM WORLD CHAMPION BOXER, CHRIS ALGIERI

Google Youngstown, Ohio. After you get through the countless stories about dilapidated steel mills and the golden age of the Industrial Revolution you're probably going to land on some cool facts about boxing. Through the decades Youngstown has produced multiple world champions. The most famous names are Ray "Boom Boom" Mancini and Kelly "The Ghost" Pavlik.

It's a town where everyone knows everyone, and everyone knows a little bit about boxing. It's also my hometown and just like the effortless pairing of a nice sweet red sauce with golden pasta noodles, nothing seems to blend quite as perfectly as a grizzled-out steel town with the romanticism of the Sweet Science (that's boxing for the uninitiated). It's fair to say I'm a combat sports junkie, I'll watch amateur MMA from Australia via livestream if that's the only game in town.

The beauty of combat lies within its honesty, two fighters, one ring, one bell, who's the better prepared athlete? Just like the first time you tasted your favourite dish at your local restaurant, boxing fans have a penchant for remembering where they were during their favourite fight; it's the thing that keeps them coming back for more. One of mine happened on June 14th, 2014, in New York City between feared Russian brawler dubbed 'The Siberian Rocky' real name: Ruslan Provodnikov, and his opponent contrastingly nicknamed 'The Collegiate' due to his education background real name: Chris Algieri.

Without turning this into a sports piece, I'll spare you the drama, but it's worth a watch, a real battle of sacrifice and effort by both men. A friend of a friend sent me Chris's contact and since then I've interviewed Algieri at least five times. This following transcript is one of those times. We can learn a lot about effort and discipline from a man who has put his life on the line via the pursuit of personal development.

The following conversation between myself and Chris Algieri took place on February 5th, 2019, while Chris was a guest on my podcast *Ungoogleable*. Chris Algieri is the former boxing WBO junior welterweight champion. Chris has been in some epic battles and has fought some huge names such as Ruslan Provodnikov, Amir Khan, Manny Pacquiao, and Errol Spence Jr. Chris is also a nutritionist and coach most notably working with Boxing Perennial Contender Danny Jacobs.

My Question: You've fought some of the biggest names in the sport, its well documented your work ethic and preparation along with the effort you put forth, can you talk a little bit about what it's like getting ready for a professional boxing match?

Chris's Answer: This past fight camp came off the heels of a two-and-a-half-year lay-off, which is a ridiculous amount of time to be off and out of the ring at this level. It feels good to be back going through the processes again going through the journey. It's not just the fights, that's what people I think don't understand; training camps are long and hard and that takes a lot out of you. You never get used to that. Then there's the ring walk, being in the back and all these things and aspects of fighting that fighters think about all the time but the people watching don't, so it was important for me to go through those processes again and get that familiar feeling again and that rumble in your gut.

Then the fights themselves; they've been perfect in the sense that I've been able to get tested and still felt like this is where I belong. I'm not done yet. I want to do this. I don't have to do this or need to do this, I don't have to box, I especially don't need to. I'm doing this because I love it. My effort put forth in my fight camps tells me all I need to know about my place in this sport. I see a spot for me here to become a world champion again.

My Question: Your fight resume is incredible; you've been in there with some of the best to ever do it. Do you ever take the time to reflect on your body of work or is that something that you don't think about?

Chris's Answer: That's a fantastic question and I've always said that things have moved so fast for me within my career. I was never kind of thinking about what was going on when it was happening, I was like, one day I'll look back on it. I did recently take time off, but I never considered myself retired, so I still really haven't looked back on my career.

I have seen what my opponents have done since then, the fact that Manny Pacquiao, I fought him five years ago now and he's still out there beating top guys. He's amazing, my adoration for him has grown so much since fighting him. He's a phenomenal athlete and such an incredible addition to the sport. Then you have Errol Spence who's one of the top five fighters in the world right now and I think eventually he's going to be number one, pound for pound. He's a stud and he's been tearing everybody apart ever since we fought, so I think a lot of my opponents maturing since I fought them shows the resume that you mentioned.

HABIT FIVE: ACTION PLAN

Your body will tell you everything you need to know about yourself if you choose to listen. I'm convinced that there's a direct connection with daily effort and overall happiness. Maybe this is psychological, but I know that I feel my best when I've challenged myself physically, this is something that I truly believe in. Your daily physical effort plays a vital role with how you view the world. Any lifestyle changes will be some of the hardest things you'll ever do. Seek out advice and guidance. Don't be afraid to ask for help and find freedom in the unknown.

It's normal to feel intimidated with a new journey so embrace it and don't push back. Start small. Today you will go for a walk and tomorrow you will do the same. Next week add five minutes of stretching before and after your walk and before you know it you've created a new healthy pattern of behaviour. Keep it simple and put in the effort.

I used to shy away from the word potential because I wasn't living up to mine. Find ways today to create something, just like you and I just created your Walk & Stretch Program you have the ability to do that with all areas of your life. It doesn't have to be grandiose. We are meant to create things, right? Or do we just consume while we're here? On earth I mean, what if our mental stability depended on us creating things and living a productive life was the key to fulfilment? Is that possible? Are you capable of creating?

CHAPTER SIX

HABIT SIX: CREATE DON'T CONSUME

WHAT IS PRODUCTIVITY?

Productivity: NOUN: The state or quality of being productive.
The effectiveness of productive effort especially in terms of sources, as measured by the rate of output per unit of input.

'Our duty as humans is to create culture, not consume culture'
— Terence McKenna[13]

Now I'm really showing my true colours; who uses a quote from a famous psychedelic explorer to drive home a point about living a productive life? You guessed right if you said me; I do. We can psychoanalyse McKenna's words all we want. We can frame them as most would who are familiar with his work and focus on consciousness and the psychedelic realm or we can take them literally and use them to align very specific paralleled meanings that are occurring daily around every single one of us.

He spoke these words in the late 1980s before the internet was mainstream. Long before smart phones were put in our pockets and replaced our best friends, McKenna was teaching

---

13   Terence McKenna 14. (1992). Archaic Revival. HarperOne. p. 242.

us about the positive role that creating plays on us both culturally and individually. A man wise beyond his years, he understood the negative consequences that arise when we, the individual, carelessly hand away our valuable time to products, entertainment, and other outside distractions.

The downside of constant intake leads to the uprise of mental health issues. I use this quote all the time to help reign me in. I often catch myself using online apps too much like your favourite social media platforms or taking deep dives down a YouTube rabbit hole finding out about the deadliest praying mantis or the haunted black rock mountain in northern Australia. It's these words that help rescue me: CREATE DON'T CONSUME.

Our duty as humans is to create culture, not consume culture! So nice I've said it twice. These words are powerful. Terence McKenna was not a man who embraced the healthy side of living, well at least not physically. He was more into the things that can't be measured. Like psychedelic trips, wood elves that appear during a DMT trip, and even out of body experiences fuelled by the power from the mushroom or more specifically, the chemical compound found in magic mushrooms called psilocybin.

I highly recommend the book *Food of the Gods* written by McKenna. I won't spoil the party, but if you're into alternative ways of thinking, especially around the origins of human existence and the advent of technology, then go read that book. It'll leave you thinking highly controversial ideas formulated by Terence most likely during an altered state of consciousness.

How is this relevant, you ask? Its relevant because after I read it, for the first time in my life, I thought to myself, *damn, there really are no rules for our individual freedoms of thought.* The book is so far out there it left me feeling empowered. If you're like me or was raised in a traditional western household with passed down customs and belief systems, then there's probably been times in your life when you've been faced with similar situations. Are these practices and schools of thought accurate? And just because my parents told me so, should I continue to think this way?

When you reach this moment, it can be both confronting and empowering. I experienced a huge mental shift in how I approached the things I read, the things I thought I believed in, along with a renewed focus around the energy I put forth throughout my day.

What an interesting perspective it is; create, don't consume. In relation to the habits, that we've covered thus far, we can all admittedly answer 'yes' to the question, 'Have we created anything today?' Let's recap, we've tossed out our snooze button, that is the creation of a new habit. We've made our bed, we've realigned our outlook on breakfast, we've reframed our perspective on the foods we eat, and we've chosen to partake in a new fitness and wellness routine. Holy shit! We've created a lot so far and the day isn't even over yet.

You see my point? To be happy, healthy, and fulfilled we don't need to seek out grandiose outcomes like being famous or having power over people. Happiness lies within us. It's not a place you can visit or an object you can touch. It's an outcome of our habits. We create it. A close friend of mine, more like a mentor, shook me to my core one day during a project we both were working on. We came together as storytellers with the common goal of filming a documentary. We had all the required variables in place to ensure that our story would be properly captured, a topic and a plan of attack; what we didn't have was a camera.

Our quest started on the ground floor as they say, considering neither one of us had ever filmed a documentary before we began by reaching out to our network and asking questions about what specific gear we needed to buy. The list was quite extensive; we shopped for cameras, camera lenses, audio equipment, microphones, lapel mics, boom mics, headphone and tripods. Once we felt comfortable with the gear, we started planning travel dates along with reaching out to potential guests to interview as well as organising hotels, rental agencies and even contacting Hollywood production companies. Over a two-year span we travelled from Sydney to LA to Myanmar and even went to the tiny magical island Cyprus. It wasn't until after we finished filming that I learned this most valuable lesson.

We were settling back into our lives in Sydney and I called him and asked about the content we filmed and the next step of our journey as filmmakers. He picked up the phone and was in a bit of a rush and asked to call me back, he says 'Hey Jonny, I'm busy now with this film editing class I'll call you back after.'

I say, 'Cool, call me when you're free' (I should mention, my friend is a successful self-made entrepreneur and could easily hire someone to do the editing of the film). I was under the impression that we were going to outsource the editing.

He rings me back and he says, 'Outsource the editing? Of course we will, we're not editors, but I want to learn how to edit first before I pay someone to do it for me. How will I be able to tell if his work is good if I don't have a grasp of what I'm outsourcing?' He then finished his statement with, 'It's a basic human fundamental.' In that moment, aspects of my worldview changed.

A statement that my buddy probably doesn't even remember shook me so deep. His words were so clear because his perspective of creating to learn, not creating to earn, was exactly what I was philosophically missing in my life at that time. Since then, not instantly but over time I adjusted from being a person who views the world as an audience member, to a person who is engaged, takes part, creates. It doesn't require any physical variables to make this shift, it's literally a mental perspective. Create. Don't consume.

Let me ask you an honest question: how old are you? I bet if you're in your thirties, forties, or older, you probably have gone years or decades without tapping into the creative side of your personality. The parts of our brain strictly related to self-worth and responsible for either how bad or how good we feel about ourselves.

When's the last time you created something? Maybe a drawing or a poem? Wanting to create things doesn't mean you want to become a famous painter or a famous singer. It also doesn't mean you want to gain a huge following online because of the movies you make, or the books you write. All this means is you're tapping into the parts of your brain that enables you to be creative. This is a very important daily habit that most people skip.

In this part of your day, to revisit the 'self-reflection' task I spoke about earlier. It's important to identify what you enjoy doing both mentally and physically. If you like to write, prioritise time every day for you to write. If you like to problem solve, then give yourself time every day to work on problems that need answering. These tasks may sound simple and mundane but unbeknownst to you is the relevance they have on your self-worth.

The easiest task can lead to the biggest breakthroughs. We feel better about the day when we are creating things. Write a poem, write a song, or simply write down your weekly chore list. The action of writing is a creative task, the value lies within the awareness of the individual who identifies this "simple" action as valuable.

Watching TV is an action of consuming. It holds zero psychological currency due to the absence of creating. We acknowledge watching TV holds no positive weight within our day, but we do it habitually. Why? Same goes with purchasing items at shops or online. You may receive an instant feeling of gratitude but it's not one of the healthier kinds. The momentary feeling of happiness is your mind playing tricks on you, it's the same high you get when you take a mind-altering drug. It's a chemical reaction in the brain caused by the physical action and impulse; it's not tangible or relevant to happiness. This feeling fades quickly and you are left wanting more. Consuming doesn't lead to happiness.

Brainstorm a list of the things you enjoyed doing when you were a kid. What were they? Did they make you happy? Can you still do them now? Maybe it's dancing; if so, when's the last time you danced? Maybe it's singing, do you still belt out the lyrics of your favourite songs? Was it writing? How long has it been since you picked up a pen and told a story? For me, it's boxing. This is how I achieve and spark my creative flow.

I do it in the forms of shadow boxing, jumping rope and occasionally sparring with clients. I also have a heavy bag hanging in my garage and if you follow me on social media, you're probably bored with all the boxing videos I share. It's not just the health benefits I receive from the physical side of things but equally as important are the benefits from the mental side of things as well. When I'm boxing, I'm my child-self, I'm free in these moments.

When we're being creative, we're free. We're no longer attached to the slavery of our day or the discourse of our careers or our bosses telling us there's a deadline due. This next bit is where most people fall short in their lives. They accomplish enough throughout their day, so their bills are paid, and their families are safe and sound, their rent and mortgages get paid and the lights in the house remain on. What about the lights within us? What keeps those on? What keeps our lights on within our spirit? I believe creativity pays those bills.

WARNING, it's about to get real "WOO-WOO" but if you look at the Buddhist philosophy, they say we are all gods. We are the creators of our thoughts. Our thoughts become our reality. Therefore, we are all gods. Meaning, you have the power within you to create the life you want to live. It starts from within, from within yourself, then from within your home.

Identify a new hobby you'll start today that will allow you to be creative. Think outside the box. Remember, you don't have to tell anyone about this. You don't have to put it on social media. You don't have to share it. Implement something that forces you to move the body, make it something physical, make it something mental, whatever you do, challenge yourself and enjoy it because you'll only understand the value of the creative flow once you're in it and that's the beauty of it. You'll reach a flow state. It's like watching your favourite performer perform, maybe you're into combat and you're watching your favourite boxer or fighter and you hear them give an interview after the performance of their life and they say, 'I was just in a flow state, I was in a flow', or you're listening to your favourite author talk on a podcast and he's referencing a chapter he had written that he says is his best work and he also mentions he didn't know where the ideas were coming from, they just came to him. You don't have to be the person who changes the world to have a creative flow. All you must do is create. There's power in the unknown.

Stop scrolling so much on social media. Either get in or get out. Your mental health is directly related to your daily productivity. Your subconscious self expects you to be active, it's why you feel down on yourself when you're lazy. Think about how you feel when you give someone you care about a gift? It makes you feel whole, you feel wanted and loved. Nobody gave you that feeling, you created it through the kind action of giving. You have the power to constantly recreate this feeling on many different scales.

INTERVIEW HIGHLIGHTS FROM ENTREPRENEUR, INVENTOR, AND STRENGTH SPECIALIST, CHRIS "THE MAD SCIENTIST" DUFFIN

During my day to day grind I'm in the health and wellness space. You already know how loud and confusing this area can be with information and so-called experts seemingly coming at us from every angle. Because of this, I'm very careful about who I learn from and who I interview. I can honestly say that the short list of humans that I call mentors and friends are the best at what they do and the most ethical about how they go about their business.

One of my go to guys in the space of strength and conditioning is the highly sought out Phil Daru. Phil is a former collegiate athlete turned professional MMA fighter turned sports scientist. Because of his extensive background in human performance his clientele base consists of famous entertainers, world class athletes, combat sports champions as well as ordinary people like you and me. When Phil talks people listen.

A while ago he reached out to me with a reference and thought that his buddy Chris, an American Strength expert, entrepreneur and author, would be a great fit for my podcast. I did my research on Chris, instantly became enamoured by his plight and life's journey and acted on Phil's excellent recommendation and set up an interview.

The following conversation between myself and Chris Duffin took place on February 1st, 2021, while Chris was a guest on my podcast *Ungoogleable*:

My Question: [One] of my favourite things about what you do, what you've done, and how you convey your messaging to the public, is the breaking down of stereotypes. The old mindset of being a strength coach, was more about how much can you lift? How many macros a day are you eating? You're a meathead, right? You're one dimensional, right? But in all your body of work Chris, it's literally what I strive to do and how I vision my daily output and productivity to be is multidimensional, like yourself. My goal is to challenge the way people think and change the way certain aspects of health and wellness are perceived. On that note, with all your successes, why are you so willing to give so much of that away?

Chris's Answer: My message is always about extremely potent thoughts, experiences and ideas. I think it's important to frame what "strength" is and it is something that we think about as going into the gym and getting big and strong but it's about resilience. It's about being able to take on stress and adapt and become a stronger and more resilient person so that you're less likely to be injured and your able to overcome the obstacles that are in your future and yeah, "physical" is a part of that. You don't want to fall and break a hip, but we also must think about the emotional, the mental or even the spiritual aspects of this. Every element is just as important. Just because my companies and much of my work is in the physical space, I also wrote a book to articulate those other messages and use stories to create another framework to share other philosophies around introspection, and how to look at how to set goals and actualise those.

My Question: Everything must count? That's kind of a message of yours as well, people taking days for granted and so many people think that tomorrow will always be there, I'll just wait until tomorrow? Everything that I've come across so far about your brand is super-efficient on that end… advice on that note?

Chris's Answer: Yeah, it's about understanding that cleaning up all the things that are not useful, that are not extraneous. We do that in the physical aspect with the tools that we create, with the coaching that we produce but also in our philosophy of life. It's really understanding, why do you want the things that you do? Hey, I want to be a stockbroker, or an NFL player, or I want to be a doctor, or I want to have a fancy house, or car, but why do you want these things? Diving deeper and understanding those things will help, and you'll get to this point of goals not being 'things' but 'words' like creativity, challenge, recognition, those are going to be the things that you can look at and apply in so many ways that you can express those, so your goal setting process really starts to change because you need to make sure that everything that you are doing ensures you that you are moving a little bit forward, ahead in your development.

HABIT SIX: ACTION PLAN

The day I truly understood what I was meant to be doing with my time was a beautiful moment in my journey. This doesn't happen by chance; it takes many conversations with yourself to get down to the crux of one's purpose. This mattered to me, and if it matters to you then be diligent about this process. The point I'm getting at is, for you to build a full comprehension of what your strengths are in relation to your goals. Once I identified 'coaching' and helping myself first to help others, I then was able to see what my process and output should look like: every day I must work out, every day I must help at least one person, and every day I must help myself in such a way that I can then pay that forward by helping others.

These personal daily tasks of mine are aligned, they are congruent, with my skills and goals. That's the key with being productive, not just being busy for the sake of it but executing tasks that will have a direct benefit to your life today or your life in the future. That, in my eyes, is true productivity. It's imperative you identify what you want, why you want it, what you are good at, then combine all those action items and start working at it.

CHAPTER SEVEN

HABIT SEVEN: ADD VALUE

WHAT IS ENRICHMENT?

Enrichment: NOUN: the action of improving or enhancing the quality or value of something or someone.

'We're so engaged in doing things to achieve purposes of outer value that we forget about our inner value, the rapture that is associated with being alive is what it is all about'
— Joseph Campbell

How many people do you know that are living lives based on other people's expectations of them? Their parents told them to go to that school, so they went. Their teachers told them to study that field at university, so they did. I'm not saying it's bad to take advice from people who care about you, I'm just saying, how can it be possible that other people know us better than we know ourselves?

I started pondering this concept a few years back when I was going through some difficult times at work with my colleagues. I was coming home miserable and was really starting to hate my job and career. I'll never forget the conversation I had with an old roommate when he started telling me about the negative side of expectations and how mentally damning they can be. I was telling him about my problems with a certain group of coaches and how my frustration had grown to such a heightened state that during one specific altercation I almost resorted to violence. It was that bad.

These guys were getting under my skin to such a personal depth that I started to feel hopeless. At the time, I figured fighting was my only option. I'm not going to get into the semantics of the petty bullshit drama, let's just say I felt betrayed and used. Put it this way: has there ever been a time in your life in which you've devoted so much energy into something or someone and that same level of commitment wasn't reciprocated? Do you remember how that made you feel? This is exactly what I was going through.

I had created realities in my mind about how people and colleagues should treat me, based on my own personal code of ethics. That night, as my roommate grasped the content of my problems and gave me the greatest piece of practical advice any friend had ever given me. He simply said, 'Hey Stofko, what I would do if I were you, which would be in your best interest, is the next time you go to work remove all the expectations you've created for others around how they should be treating you. These people you work with don't owe you anything so don't oblige them by thinking that they do.' This made so much sense to me. More powerful words have never been spoken.

I'm not sure if you guys have ever experienced a real life 'Ah-hah' moment, but I have, and this was one of them. In that moment my roommate, Jesse, had helped shift my perspective on things. I understood what he was saying right away. Just because

I hold myself to certain standards and morals don't mean that other people do, and that's okay. Placing expectations on people in relation to how they should be treating you isn't fair for me, or the parties involved.

Over the next few months, I started noticing changes at my job. Rather than engaging in toxic conversations and base level chit chat, I avoided it all together. Initially, I felt isolated but over time I became aware of what was happening. Once I started removing the expectations along with the banter I used to partake in, I started seeing a change in my mental health while I was at work. I started becoming more independent and more aware of what I now needed.

My issue all along wasn't reciprocation, it was enrichment. I needed empowering conversations that suited my mindset, so I made a commitment to myself. I'd rather have no friends, than a group of friends that don't add value. This works both ways. I can't be at my best either if I'm surrounding myself with people who allow me to be toxic towards them. I began a quest of awareness, of sorts. My mental checklist surrounding all my personal relationships began with the same two thoughts: *1) Does this person add value to my life?* And *2) What value do I add to theirs?*

I almost forgot; I need to tell you guys a little bit about the author of the quote. Let me first show you a few of my favourite quotes and see if you recognise any of them:

The cave you fear to enter holds the treasure you seek.

Follow your bliss and the universe will open doors for you where there were only walls.

If you're unfamiliar with Campbell, he's the guy who coined the phrase 'The Hero's Journey' in comparison to one's life.

He became quite famous because of his philosophies, so famous that it's probably fair to say every single one of your modern favourite Hollywood movies has been impacted and designed based on Campbell's 'Hero's Journey' philosophy.

My laypersons' explanation goes as follows: the hero is announced in the story, then there's a call to adventure, some type of supernatural aid occurs, he's then faced with major challenges and temptations, there's a death or a rebirth usually of the ego, a revelation or breakthrough happens, then a transformation, followed by atonement, then finalised by a 'full circle' closure of return.

Campbell's perspective on adding value is one of my favourites. He talks about quite often the fact of the only way we can truly reach the heightened state of fulfilment is by fulfilling oneself; we must add value to our own life for us to be of value to those who are in our lives. I love the deep talk and the introspective philosophies of those who came before me.

How does this all tie in? The answer is simple: how much of your day is spent adding value to yourself? How much of it is spent adding value to others? Finally, how much of it is spent by your so-called "friends" and "acquaintances" adding value to your life? Once you figure this equation out you will then begin the process of applying the 'add value' habit to your day that so many successful and productive humans subscribe to.

Here's how I attack this: My daily action plan always consists of prioritising the seeking out of enriched conversations. Nothing base level, meaning I no longer waste valuable time gossiping about people I know or talking about meaningless celebrity bullshit. On the other hand, my interactions don't necessarily need to be life changing, they just need to be something honest that speaks to my truest intentions as well as my spirit. I gain this from the people I choose to have in my life. You will gain this from the people you choose to have in yours, whether it's your kids, your parents, your friends, your roommates or whoever else happens to play a role within your day to day.

You can easily test this out. Tomorrow, at your job, search for only enriched conversations and create boundaries around them. Don't settle for the normal 'How's the weather?' or 'Did you catch that game last night?' conversations. Challenge your peers and colleagues to go deeper, and if they can't then you don't and simply move forward.

In depth and powerful conversations require vulnerability from both sides. Never undervalue the importance of being vulnerable and always be aware of the consequences of engaging or continuing toxic conversations and relationships. The highest form of enriched communications are solely the outcome relationships that are built on trust and vulnerability. These communications lead to moments of inspiration and help promote progress and development.

We also must be aware of the difference between motivated individuals and those who are driven. There's a very important contrast between the person who lives a driven life, versus the person who relies on motivation. Never strive to be motivated. These are the people who start something but never finish it. I call them 'ask holes'. We all know someone who constantly asks us for life advice, but they never act upon the advice given. They continuously make the same mistakes repeatedly.

Don't listen to motivational speakers, don't seek out motivational videos and schemes; they're like a drug. They are external, they're fleeting. The motivational speaker will give you a quick little hit, a buzz. It's a drug, they are drug dealers, dealing in hormones and impulse. The feelings are due to chemicals in the brain called dopamine and serotonin. Then the show ends, and the stage lights are dark, you go back to your car, and you start to drive home. You're feeling great but shortly you realise the vibe has worn off. What are you left with? Have you learned any applicable skills from the speaker? Have you learned the secrets they promised would help you positively impact your life and assist you with turning your life around? Hell no, you didn't learn anything. They gave you nothing but an impulse.

Motivation is like fishing in a lake with just your hands and no reel or hooks and when you finally grab a fish, you pull it out of the water, but it jumps out of your hands. In the end, all you're left with are the scales, those scales are the equivalent to motivation.

Now let's talk about the person who is driven. These people don't believe in motivational speakers and secret groups and chants. They believe in themselves. They've worked on themselves tirelessly to develop healthy habits that directly benefit their day to day lives. Being driven becomes ingrained in your DNA. Somebody who is driven doesn't need a motivational speaker to inspire them; they know who they are because they've identified what they're good at, they've listed out what their goals are, and they surround themselves around the people who care about them the most. Being driven is internal, it's intrinsic, nobody can take this away from you. It is an outcome of your processes and daily habits.

A driven person is a result of all of the conversations they've had every single day with everyone in their lives. Now look, I understand, you might be working in a job, and you don't get along with everyone. I've been there before, you have options. You might not even get along with your roommate but what you can do today is start out by challenging the conscious thought between you and that person. Create boundaries around the topics you speak about with your co-workers and friends. It's better to say nothing than to engage in a base level conversation that leaves you second guessing yourself, that leaves you second guessing your own path and mission and leaves you uninterested.

Demand more of yourself and more from those who you choose to be closely connected to you and your daily life. Are you familiar with the Buddhist philosophy on sexual and intimate partners? When I first learned about this it changed my perspective forever, on not only those who I choose to be intimate with, but also those who I choose to spend the most time around. It goes, 'Be aware of the people you have sex with. You not only leave a piece of you with them, but you also take a piece of them away with you.' So much value, right?

Givers gain. In a world that's easily viewed as designed for the takers, you will find your value by adding value to others. You don't need to expect anything in return. Nor does value necessarily need to be in the form of objects or gifts. Gestures also do the trick. Say hello to the older woman crossing the road, hold the elevator for the gentleman on level eight. Value comes in all forms and once you figure this out you will begin to see it everywhere.

INTERVIEW HIGHLIGHTS FROM PROFESSIONAL ATHLETE, MIXED MARTIAL ARTIST, AND MULTIPLE TIME WORLD CHAMPION AUNG LA N SANG

Think about something you're good at. Maybe it's something you excelled at when you were younger, as a child even. Did you ever win your school's spelling bee? Maybe you made your little league All Star team. Hold on, I know something, you made the Honour Roll before in High School, right? You might even have a college degree. Whatever your accomplishments may be, however big, or small, these are all significant moments in time that permanently became bookmarked within your life.

Let's play a game, pick one of your most memorable moments and imagine that because your achievement was so significant your hometown decided to erect a lifelike, bronze statue in the middle of your town square to honour you. You're asking yourself, surely these public acknowledgements happen posthumously, and because of that, you'll never actually experience that sort of attention and notoriety.

So, imagine that you're alive and well, in the heart of your chosen career and you get notified that your hometown, specifically in your honour is going to construct a bronze statue of you for the whole world to see simply to acknowledge your achievements? Sounds like a movie, right? Wrong. This is the positive impact professional mixed martial artist and multiple time world champion Aung La N Sang has left on his people. It's difficult for someone like me to try and comprehend the multitude of levels of pressure that this gesture comes with.

I was introduced to Aung La N Sang years ago, by mutual friends; he is a Burmese born professional athlete and a multiple time world champion in the sport of mixed martial arts. I've had the pleasure to work with, interview and get to know one of the most impressive people I've ever come across. In his world, family comes above everything so what better person to learn from in relation to enrichment and the idea of living with purpose then Aung La.

The following conversation between myself and Aung La N Sang took place on May 20th, 2020, while Aung La was a guest on my podcast *Ungoogleable:*

My Question: What does it mean to you to have an entire nation, your home country of Myanmar revere you at such a high level? More importantly, first, with the whole world recently being locked down due to COVID, how are you handling everything and how do you maintain a positive mindset, where does that come from?

Aung La's Answer: I'm good. I'm well, just hanging out with my family. [Lockdown has] been good to me, you know? Everything has stopped. The whole world has stopped but I haven't. I've been training a lot and staying ready for what is supposed to be an upcoming fight. Knowing of where I am, and knowing of what I've been through and where I came from, it's been everything to me. Staying positive comes from my coaches, my team, my country, and my family. I'm fighting for not just myself or not just my family now, I'm fighting for my fans, my friends and my family back home in Myanmar. People of all ages back home who support me and show me their continued support gives me so much energy and it gives me so much happiness for what I'm doing right now. You have little kids cheering for me then you have older ladies and older men cheering for me as well. I have an amazing audience, so I must make the most out of it.

My Question: Even though you are in America, you still have this impact in Myanmar; what does that mean to you?

Aung La's Answer: My goal is to eventually bring over all sorts of talent from Myanmar. Right now, I work with a handful of athletes, I'm kind of using them as a 'Test run' to have them train martial arts. They do love martial arts, they love MMA, but I want them to master Myanmar's sport first, 'Lethwei' because that's our tradition, that's who we are and so these kids are training Lethwei. They are going to school as well, a couple of them are from the IDP camps (Internally Displaced Refugee Camps) and some of them are from the city that I grew up in and some of them are from other places, but I want these kids, these young kids to have a future, have a future in combat sports and be able to take care of themselves. What happens right now is that the young kids feel hopeless, so they get into drugs and that bothers me. I hate that feeling for them, I want them to have an outlet. I want them to work hard, be dedicated and be disciplined. That's what I'm trying to teach them.

HABIT SEVEN: ACTION PLAN

You can always do more. Helping others, giving compliments to strangers and practising what you preach is how you become enriched daily. It seems cheesy but it's not, there's real benefit to this. Enrichment can be gained with little to no effort. Focus on being kind and not settling for the "normal" reaction to moments that may disappoint. During the day, learn to slow things down during moments of stress and anxiety, take a breath and ask yourself, 'how can I react to this differently?'

This question will serve you in more ways than you know.

Having a daily purpose that's aligned with your code of ethics, principles, habits and goals is a great way to be fulfilled. You just heard what Aung La said, right? He's a guy who's a trained assassin and could injure any human severely with his bare hands but all he talks about is helping people, why is that? You got it, he's enriched, his days are filled with actions that positively impact himself and his family so he's able to have his thoughts and intentions aligned with many positive ideations.

You don't have to be a pro athlete with a statue of yourself to positively make a difference. It starts with filling your glass first. Reaching your potential depends strictly on reaching for your goals first then you'll be in a better position to wear yourself thin. Help yourself so you can help others.

Waking up in the morning and feeling great about your mind and body is very possible, no matter how long it's been for you since you've been healthy or how long you think it's going to take for you to see results. Not getting started on the path of being healthy due to your unknown worries about the effort of the journey is a fallacy.

Don't allow the trickery of the unknown to deter you from moving forward. Can you answer this question truthfully, don't speak it aloud, speak it to yourself: Are you healthy? Are you vital? Have you put your body, your mind and your immune system in the best possible situation to be able to fight off infection? Have you earned it? Be honest with yourself, how's your vitality? Have you put in the required work for you to be able to answer confidently Yes, that if you got seriously ill today that you'd be able to fully recover? Is vitality a word you think about or even care about? Do you think your family, your kids, your loved ones, those who rely on you, do you think they care about your vitality?

CHAPTER EIGHT

HABIT EIGHT: SLEEP WELL

WHAT IS VITALITY?

Vitality: NOUN: the state of being strong and active. It's the energy that's pulsing through, the power giving continuance of life, present in all living things.

'Almost everything, all external possessions, all pride, all fear of embarrassment or failure, these things just fall away in the face of death, leaving only what is truly important. Remembering that you are going to die is the best way I know to avoid the trap of thinking you have something to lose. You are already naked. There is no reason not to follow your heart.'
— Steve Jobs[14]

People often say the greatest lessons in life are those learned through sorrow and pain. My life experiences have taught me this. Watching my father wither away in the span of six months is the hardest thing I've ever had to go through. I was twenty-seven at the time and was living a life devoid of meaning and purpose. I'm not going to sit here and say it was strictly my father's death that enabled me to better understand life, but I will say it was

---

14   Steve Jobs (2005), in his Stanford Commencement Address

the catalyst for my own inquiry into seeking out my purpose and questioning what the hell is going on in this reality. His death came out of nowhere and then, just like that, he was gone.

The memories I value the most aren't the ones of him sick and trapped in a hospital during his last days, but the moments we shared when he didn't realise I was even watching him. For months I would fly home back and forth between California and Ohio to visit. One trip he'd seem fine, and life would seem normal, but on other trips he'd be hospitalised and the sadness was so heavy it would paint the walls of my parent's house a greyish metallic colour.

This emotional rollercoaster ride finally came to an end in the middle of March while I was visiting him at the hospice. This was a 'end of life' home, a place designed for those who were in their last days on earth. This was a very confusing and numbing time for me.

I remember one moment at the hospice vividly. My father was outside in this little park area that had been decorated with colourful plants and handcrafted wooden ornament style bird feeders. He didn't know I had arrived yet. I stood, looking through a window, watching him for nearly a half hour as he stared intensely at the trees and plants. He gazed at the sky, looking eerily peaceful and calm. That's when I realised, he still hadn't told me he was dying.

I'd known he was dying for the last six months. Throughout all my visits with him, we'd watch baseball games together, we'd share our opinions about the upcoming sporting seasons, but even with all these visits and long conversations, he never once told me he was dying. More importantly, he never once turned to me and asked, 'Why me?'

I'll never forget how my dad handled his death sentence. Of course, he knew he was dying, the doctors told him when he was first admitted to the hospital, but he never brought it up to me. Then again, I never asked. We both knew what was going on.

The dignity I learned in those days will stay with me forever. Death is often depicted in movies as the saddest moment in the script. You often hear cries of desperation and echoes of sorrow and despair. Maybe I was expecting that. Maybe it would have made more sense if my father was crying out and asking, 'Why me?' but he wasn't.

At his best, he was a big, strong and proud man. Despite the guy everyone knew as a charming and charismatic figure, he was also very introverted and liked spending time by himself. I wish this was the part where I tell you that he'd lived a life full of enrichment, surpassed his potential, and that he accomplished everything he set out to do, but I'd be lying. Sometimes life doesn't pan out how we envision it, and he passed away with so much more to give.

Every day, my father's death serves as a reminder that talent is worthless without action. Potential is only a perspective and holds no value without the effort to fuel it. I loved my dad and I think about him all the time. My drive is fuelled by the lesson of impermanence that I sadly learned via his passing.

Every day, I wake up and I tell myself that one day I'm going to die. This isn't supposed to sound morbid and I'm not trying to be nihilistic, I mean it when I tell you death inspires me. We all die. If this wasn't the case, then I'd probably have a different stance. If the rich kids got to stay forever due to their family's financial status, then hell yeah, I'd be pissed off about dying, but because of the cyclical nature of life and its ultimate outcome, death does inspire me. Damn! We got deep again, didn't we? Talk about meaningful conversations and vulnerability, right?

The best way for me to explain my outlook on potential is to compare my daily output to a ripened orange. When it's ready, the orange provides a sweet, nutrient dense cocktail of natural energy, left un-squeezed, the orange will rot and go to waste. My goal is to always approach my day with the mindset of squeezing that orange as much as I can to ensure I won't be wasting anything. I mentioned this earlier in the book; when you start implementing these habits into your daily routine, they change you. It's impossible to revert to your former self. Here we are now, at the author of the quote, Steve Jobs. He's a man who helped spearhead the technological revolution and connect the world through his little metal and glass inventions. In 2007, when the first iPhone was released, I wonder if anyone knew at the time how much smaller the world had instantly become. Through its release, the public received an invention that connected people all over the world.

Give me some time and I'll come full circle with this chapter's title and its action word "vitality". You must be thinking to yourself, *How the hell does any of this connect to sleep or vitality?* Here's your answer: In 2005, I was twenty-three years old and was starting to be a little more interested in bigger picture ideas. I was at my local library checking my emails when I noticed a message from an old college friend. The subject read: watch this. It was a video of a tech CEO giving a speech at a university commencement ceremony.

Normally, I would've just deleted the email but because it was sent from a credible and studious friend of mine, I chose to click the link and listen. Steve Job's speech left a huge impact on my growing perspective on life and death.

In his speech he tells a few very important stories about his journey through life. He talks about his experiences at Reed College, the lessons he learned from things not working out for him there. He mentions a story about young love and how his obsession with growing his ideas took from him the opportunity to fall deeply in love with a woman that he cared about. He then transitions into the part where he was fired by his own company, the very company he helped create turned to him and told him to leave, that his services weren't needed anymore. He talks about the powerful lessons learned through his failures and the importance those shortcomings hold in regard to not giving up and using the insights to progressively grow. As his speech is winding down, he discusses his recent cancer diagnosis and how it's sometimes confusing for him to not know how much time he has left on earth to accomplish all of the goals that he's set out to achieve.

The speech itself is great, it's very moving and honest, but those aren't the reasons why I personally love it. For me I see a dying man who's come to terms with his flaws, I hear a man who recognises albeit in his final moments all the things that he took for granted. On that stage he's not a pioneer tech wizard who's on the cusp of changing the world but simply a teacher, a man with wisdom who in the moment recognises his last opportunity to pay it forward.

Without even hearing that speech, everyone reading probably recognises his sign off. Before he puts the microphone down one last time and exits the stage he says, 'Stay Hungry. Stay Foolish. Thank you all very much.'

I've watched and read these words many times over. How do

we reach a point in our lives that allows us to positively impact people? How do we positively impact ourselves? The answer to both questions can be found in the same room where this book started. Strength arises when we sleep, allowing our minds and bodies to recover from a stressful day.

Why do so many of us avoid conversations about sleep health? Are we too busy to sleep? If so, how do we reconcile the two? You lived a whole day, you get home, you have put your healthy routine of habits in place over the last twelve hours, enabling you to become a better version of yourself. These habits have allowed you to remain calm with a clear and level-headed perspective. You have not been sucked dry from toxic relationships, your body isn't feeling fatigued from being lethargic or lazy. Your body is tingly from working out, your mind is sparked from the enriched conversations you have had and now you're getting ready to lay your head on your pillow and call it a day.

This may be the most important part of your day. There used to be this old way of thinking around the exact number of hours of sleep a person needs each night to be healthy and productive the next day. There actually isn't a specific amount of quantity that's needed. Scientists used to say you need eight or ten hours. We now know this is all bullshit. All the new research suggests quality over quantity[15].

Are we achieving REM sleep? REM stands for: Rapid Eye Movement. The amount of time spent in this state is super beneficial. Our bodies run on a circadian rhythm, aligned with all living things on earth. It's interesting what happens to our bodies when we achieve regulatory sleep patterns. Risk of degenerative

---

15 Sleep duration and mortality: a systematic review and meta-analysis

brain diseases highly decrease. New studies suggest a link between Alzheimer patients and sleep deprivation[16].

I'm not going to tell you how many specific hours a night to sleep, I'm not going to tell you too long or too short, what I *am* going to tell you is that there's value in regulating your sleep patterns.

The quicker we design a game plan, Monday through Sunday of going to bed at the same time and waking up at the same time, the quicker we can get our health back on track. Regulatory sleep patterns have been known to not only boost your energy levels but also provide benefits to your mental health. The worst thing you can do is mentally "clock out" come Friday afternoon. Just because the work week ends, doesn't mean your daily systems and habits must end.

Stop compartmentalising your weekends from your health and wellbeing and start prioritising your daily habits. You think your body differentiates what day it is? You think it's healthy to eat clean and live a healthy and active lifestyle Monday through Friday but then on the weekends you drink to get drunk? So many people look forward to the weekends, because on Saturdays or Fridays, they think they can act as if there are no consequences.

Every day is every day. Saturday is not an excuse for you to eat shit. Saturday is not an excuse for you to have an all-nighter. Create systems and patterns that you use on Mondays that you are still going to use on Saturdays. As a result, over time as we get older, our body's systems are going to be healthier. I challenge you to create a boundary with when you go to bed and create a

---

16 Authors: Zhang, X., Giovannucci, E., Wu, K., Gao, X., Hu, F., & Ogino, S. Published: in JAMA Network Open, 2019

boundary with when you wake up. Focus on going to bed at the same time every night and focus on waking up at the same time every day.

I have said this before, nobody is perfect, and you are going to have good and bad days. These eight habits you now have are a matrix within a system. You have boundaries, you have achievable, sustainable habits you've created. I'm not telling you to go out and buy the latest technology on biomechanics. You don't have to join a gym; you don't have to hire a coach. All you must do is take ownership in your own health and wellness. You're learning easily achievable and applicable steps that you'll be able now to teach your parents, your friends, your children, and that you'll be able to use throughout the rest of your life.

These habits work when you are on holiday, when you are vacationing. Every single day, there is no excuse that these habits cannot be intertwined within your day to day. I'm proof of the benefits. You are going to feel better, you are going to have more energy, your body is going to look better, your mind is going to be sharper, relationships with people are going to be more enriched. There's going to be more value and opportunities presented to you. It's that famous quote, 'Our net worth is our network.' We create this reality through the conversations we have and through the relationships we nurture. You now have a plan of attack with your time. You're no longer being pulled in all directions.

These habits sound so rudimentary, yet so many people don't practise them. What's going to be your excuse? Isn't that the definition of insanity? Continuously doing something over and over and expecting different results.

Regulating your sleep patterns won't take a ton of effort and the more consistent you are the more energy you will have. Like everything else beneficial to your livelihood, discipline and patience are vital. Live today with urgency. Live with intention and focus solely on the things that you love to do and the people that you love to do those things with.

This is the only real currency there is: the kindness you share with others along with the kindness you give to yourself. I have a special relationship with all my clients, each one requires something different. Some need mental pressure from me to corner them and they use that pressure as fuel to reach their goals, and some of them require a bit more kindness and nurturing. People are the same, yet at the same time we're all so very different. One of my clients simply needs two words from me that I tell her after every session and I'll tell you as well, love yourself.

INTERVIEW HIGHLIGHTS FROM PROFESSOR AND SCIENTIST, DR JOSE ANTONIO

In preparation for this book, I compiled hundreds of interviews both for my podcast and for my own personal development. Back in 2018 I had yet to publish my first book, let alone starting to think about this one. As time passed, my intentions shifted. In my digital content I went from solely focusing on person-to-person interviews, to having a deep intrigue with writing and storytelling.

I wasn't choosing guests to interview based on future ideas about key points or references inside chapters of a future book. It's really been an organic process. Sometimes I'll interview a guest and never share it, other times I'll take the same interview and distribute it in various ways, such as a podcast, a blog, or a YouTube video. As my journey continues and my experience grows, I perceive my output not only as lessons for myself but also opportunities to help others.

When I was working on which interviewee would pair the best with this chapter, it was clear to me that a guest who not only practices what they preach, but more importantly has the body of work to back up their message, would be the only fit. A person with a lifelong journey of research, of health and wellness, and more precisely vitality would be the only way to go here. The daily actions we displayed yesterday dictate how well we live tomorrow.

Dr Jose Antonio is the co-founder of The International Society of Sports Science. The following conversation between myself and Dr Jose Antonio took place on November 23rd, 2020, while Jose was a guest on my podcast *Ungoogleable:*

My Question: I think it's a healthy thing to talk about, with the current global pandemic, having the conversation about not brushing our wellbeing under the rug [what are] your thoughts on that?

Jose's Answer: What's interesting is that in the US, it really depends where you live. Some places like New York City or LA, it's completely different [from] where I am in South Florida. Outside of having to wear a mask when you go into a business, you would never know anything was going on. It's pretty much business as usual, although there is something that annoys me. As you know, I do a lot of stand up paddling. Florida [has] a huge paddling scene, the number of races that are being hosted are much less, it's weird because you are on the water and almost by definition you are not even near anyone because you're on a craft. A fourteen-foot board. There's no one near you[!]

So, the races have dropped a bit. It's not like in New York City.

There's a lot of places where gyms are closed, which I'm like, holy shit, gyms are closed? What the hell? That's crazy. The one place that promotes health and vitality has been taken away from many people but to those people they will find a way to continue their healthy living due to their instilled daily habits.

My Question: When we are lazy or when we are bored, people don't like to suffer. They don't want to be uncomfortable and it's unfortunate with so many people who choose to be comfortable and unbeknownst to them, a little bit of suffering can go a long way, what are your thoughts on that?

Jose's Answer: I always say, there's got to be a little bit of discomfort in your life for you to get better, for whatever tasks you are trying to accomplish. If it's not difficult, it's almost not worth doing. Think about why people push their bodies during athletic events, why people push their brains in terms of studying a subject, so it's a requirement. You must experience discomfort, not a lot always, but a little to grow.

My Question: What role does your healthy and physical lifestyle play on your mental and academic career?

Jose's Answer: That is an amazing question, very few people put it in those terms. What's interesting is, if I go back to graduate school, when I was studying for my PhD, I did two things; either I was in the lab doing research or I was in the gym.

I was a gym rat. I love lifting but as I got older, I became much more interested in lifting to gain weight. I'm a 'hard gainer', I've always had a hard time gaining weight. When I was in grad school, I did a little self-experiment. I wanted to see if I could constantly eat and always feel full and see how much weight I could gain. I did this for three months with the goal of being full. You feel gross when you're full all day. I went from about 166 pounds to roughly 190 in three months. I think my girlfriend at the time said, 'You look like you blew up.' She said I looked like the Michelin Man, like my body was inflated with air. I got stronger but I looked and felt sluggish. I went through all these phases of self-experimentation with exercise and I think when I hit forty or forty-five, I realised that I just feel better when I work out. It's not a vanity thing. It's not a look thing. It's simply if I don't work out I feel like shit, and when I work out, I feel better.

HABIT EIGHT: ACTION PLAN

Look, it's no secret what the task at hand is. If you're unfit, you know deep down you need to make a change. The only way to feel better and feel good about you and your day is to put effort towards those goals. One of my clients once asked me, 'Jonny, I'm always tired, what can I do to have more energy on a daily basis?' I asked her, other than the twice a week you train with me, how many other days are you active and she told me none. This is a common misunderstanding, thinking that your body will magically have energy without moving it. Initially this may not make sense to you but the only way to naturally have energy is by burning energy. This is how your body works, you can't just lay around all day thinking that just because you haven't moved that you have this magical bin of stored energy. Your body requires movement to function, through this exertion is where you'll create energy. In short, move your body daily.

CONCLUSION

IN CASE YOU MISSED IT...

It doesn't matter if you've never worked out before or if you're five years into your health and wellness journey, structure is vital for any continuous success. How we measure 'success' is solely up to the individual: You.

I want everyone to understand that living a healthy lifestyle isn't easy. Think about the fast-food restaurants in your neighbourhood, are they healthy? The foods provided by restaurants aren't chosen because they're the healthiest. In America, commercials about how to live healthy lifestyles aren't broadcasted to the public but pharmaceutical ads are: Why is that?

Our general knowledge around health, fitness, and nutrition is extremely rudimentary. Most people aren't aware of the correct portion sizes, let alone understand the differences between quality of food versus quantity.

The average person has no clue of the proper methodologies of exercise. At night, we're clueless about how often we should be sleeping, let alone what healthy sleep patterns are. During our work week, how many of us understand the detrimental side effects of constant stress on the body? Are we aware of the negative consequences of being overworked? Students aren't taught these basic human fundamentals in school, hell, neither are teachers.

My point is, just do your best, along with doing your own research. It's difficult to get healthy and even harder to stay healthy, but at least now you can't say, 'I didn't know.'

These eight habits I've presented to you are applicable things I do every day that assist me in staying on track. Look at them as a daily framework and like I mentioned earlier, don't be afraid to change some things around.

Finally, be diligent about prioritising your wellness. This will encourage those around you, your loved ones, to do the same. We don't live forever, so the goal should always be to live well and to live strong.

#ISD1MF

BIBLIOGRAPHY

1. Anchorman. (2004). [Motion picture]. United States: DreamWorks Pictures.
2. Gladwell, M. (2008). Outliers: The story of success. Little, Brown and Company.
3. Aristotle. (2009). Nicomachean Ethics (W. D. Ross, Trans.). Digireads.com Publishing. (Original work published 350 BCE)
4. Dickens, C. (2018). Hard times. Oxford University Press. (Original work published 1854)
5. Willink, J. (2017). Discipline equals freedom: Field manual. St. Martin's Press.
6. McRaven, W. H. (2017). Make your bed: little things that can change your life...and maybe the world. Grand Central Publishing.
7. Watts, A. (1975). Myth and ritual in Christianity. Thames and Hudson.
8. Watts, A. (1966). The book: On the taboo against knowing who you are. Vintage Books.
9. Watts, A. (1959). The wisdom of insecurity: A message for an age of anxiety. Vintage Books.
10. Watts, A. (1951). The wisdom of insecurity: A message for an age of anxiety. Pantheon Books.

11. Watts, A. (1951). The wisdom of insecurity: A message for an age of anxiety. Pantheon Books.

12. Ziglar, Z. (1991). See you at the top. Pelican Publishing Company.

13. Gandhi, M. K. (1957). The Mind of Mahatma Gandhi. Navajivan Publishing House.

14. McKenna, T. (1992). Food of the gods: The search for the original tree of knowledge. Bantam Books.

15. Campbell, J. (1991). The power of myth. Anchor Books.

16. Campbell, J. (1949). The hero with a thousand faces. Pantheon Books.

17. Campbell, J. (1949). The hero with a thousand faces. Pantheon Books.

18. Campbell, J. (1988). The power of myth. Doubleday.

19. Campbell, J. (1991). The hero with a thousand faces. Princeton University Press.

20. Jobs, S. (2005). Stanford commencement address. Stanford University.

21. Lally, P., van Jaarsveld, C. H., Potts, H. W., & Wardle, J. (2010). How are habits formed: Modelling habit formation in the real world. European Journal of Social Psychology, 40(6), 998-1009.

22. Zhang, X., Giovannucci, E., Wu, K., Gao, X., Hu, F., & Ogino, S. (2019). "Sleep duration and mortality: a systematic review and meta-analysis" Published: in JAMA Network Open.

Shawline Publishing Group Pty Ltd
www.shawlinepublishing.com.au

SHAWLINE
PUBLISHING
GROUP

More great Shawline titles can be found by scanning the QR code below.
New titles also available through Books@Home Pty Ltd.
Subscribe today at www.booksathome.com.au or scan the QR code below.

Milton Keynes UK
Ingram Content Group UK Ltd.
UKHW021013301023
431589UK00014B/220